Praise for
Stories of Saints and the Sacraments

"When it comes to honoring the saints, Catholics are over-the-top! We love and celebrate our saints and look to them for guidance and inspiration. The saints also make wonderful teachers! In *Stories of Saints and the Sacraments,* Sister Marie Paul Curley and Sister Mary Lea Hill invite readers to learn about the sacraments from the lives of fourteen holy men and women. In addition to the engaging stories about the lives of these saints, the reader's guide included near the end of the book provides readers with reflective questions that invite us to connect the saints' lives to our lives and to the sacraments—a helpful resource for individuals and small groups to grow closer to our Lord in the most Catholic of ways."

— Joe Paprocki, author, speaker, National Consultant for Faith Formation, Loyola Press

"The power in the stories of the saints is in the seed they plant in our minds: 'If he or she can do it, then maybe I can too.' *Stories of Saints and the Sacraments* is sure to scatter those seeds into the minds of its readers and, with God's grace, help bear tremendous fruit for the Kingdom."

— Tanner Kalina, evangelist and author

"*Stories of Saints and the Sacraments* by Daughters of St. Paul Sisters Marie Paul Curley, FSP, and Mary Lea Hill, FSP, is an inspiring addition to the treasury of catechetical resources available to assist people in picturing, envisioning, and comparing a connection from the biblical word to the stories of their lives and to the kingdom of God.

In addition, at the end of each chapter there are sections for Personal Challenge and Chapter Notes that provide insights into personal reflections and applications."

— Father Brian Cavanaugh, TOR,
Franciscan University of Steubenville

Stories of Saints and the Sacraments

Stories of Saints and the Sacraments

Marie Paul Curley, FSP, and Mary Lea Hill, FSP

With a Foreword by Father John Riccardo

Pauline
BOOKS & MEDIA
BOSTON

Library of Congress Control Number: 2025934186

ISBN 10: 0-8198-1704-X

ISBN 13: 978-0-8198-1704-4

Cover art/design and interior art by www.knjms.com

Published by Pauline Books & Media, 50 Saint Paul's Avenue, Boston, MA 02130-3491

Printed in the U.S.A.

www.pauline.org

Pauline Books & Media is the publishing house of the Daughters of St. Paul, an international congregation of women religious serving the Church with the communications media.

1 2 3 4 5 6 7 8 9 30 29 28 27 26 25

For our loved ones who have gone before us
and are part of the great company of saints, especially:

Stanley R. Curley
and
Lee J. Hill

Contents

Foreword

Some years ago while in prayer I had an experience of being inside some sort of stadium. The stands were full, and everyone was wearing white. It looked and sounded like what is called a "white out" on college campuses when they host a nighttime football game. The stadium was packed, the people in the stands were cheering, and the noise was deafening, but in a very good and positive way. As the experience in prayer continued, I felt as though I heard the Lord say to me, "John, that's heaven." The Spirit quickly took me to the Letter to the Hebrews, where in chapter 12 the author compares our lives to being inside something like a stadium, "surrounded by a great cloud of witnesses," as we run the race that is the game of life.

As anyone knows who has ever been to a college football game, fans don't go to a game just to watch it; they go to help change the outcome. Thousands of cheering fans have the effect of inspiring players on the field to do things that far surpass what they could ever do on a practice field with no one watching.

This image has helped me immensely with regard to what we call "the Communion of Saints." For many Catholics, perhaps, the saints are just names from the past, people who lived long ago, but with whom we have no real interaction. Such is not the case. The saints are alive! And, like the people in the stands at a football game, they're not just watching us. The saints are, even now, cheering us on when we feel weak, interceding for us to evangelize and recreate this world as they did theirs, and eager for us to join them in the life that is to come. We are "surrounded by a great cloud of witnesses!"

In the rich pages that follow, Sister Marie Paul Curley and Sister Mary Lea Hill help us better know some of these witnesses with whom we are probably slightly familiar and learn about saints previously unknown to us. While most of us know something about the conversion and life of Saint Paul or Saint Augustine, and are aware that Saint Cecilia is the patron saint of music, I imagine few of us have ever even heard of Saint Lorenzo Ruiz or Saint Peter To Rot. When the Communion of Saints is brought to life through insightful and short biographies, we not only learn more about these heroes in our family but are also encouraged to be conscious of their mighty intercession and to call upon it more intentionally.

Even as for some Catholics the Communion of Saints can be a mere line in the Creed that we recite on Sunday, for many of us the sacraments can easily become mere rituals. This can be a great danger, especially for those of us who are ordained. Nothing is worse than getting used to the *magnificent*—and the sacraments are just that: magnificent. Oh, they are rituals, to be sure, but there is nothing "mere" about them!

Especially on the heels of the National Eucharistic Revival in our country, we are living in a time when the Church is being invited to reclaim an ever greater awareness of, and awe at, what happens when a person is baptized, confirmed, joined in holy Matrimony, anointed, ordained a ministerial priest, receives the astounding grace that is God's forgiveness, or feeds on the Body, Blood, Soul, and Divinity of Jesus in the Eucharist.

For example, Jesus gives himself to us in the Eucharist for a reason. There is something he longs to see transpire in us as we feed upon him. Unlike the other food we consume, the Eucharist breaks us down, or at least Jesus desires for this to happen in us, so that we can truly become more like what (or Whom) we eat. We receive a sacramental "blood transfusion" every time we receive Communion! His own Precious Blood rushes into our hearts, wanting and empowering them to turn from hearts of stone to hearts of flesh, and enabling us—who live in a culture and world so often filled with anger, division, resentment, and unforgiveness—to become agents of reconciliation and healing.

Saint Elizabeth Seton, as we'll see in the pages that follow, is a wondrous and hopeful example of how this happened to her and can happen in you and in me. When she entered into full communion with the Church, she experienced abandonment and betrayal by those who had been closest to her. Yet the Eucharist served not only to overwhelm her with God's intimate nearness and love for her, it also gave her the grace and strength to forgive those who had caused her so much pain. Moreover, it provided supernatural strength for setting out on the mission to which God uniquely called her.

The saints we read about in the pages that follow were destined to live when and where they did. To each of them, God gave a unique and personal mission, and their faith and the power of the sacraments enabled them to understand and faithfully carry out those missions. As it was with them, so it is with us. Nobody is alive by chance; we don't just happen to be here. Just as it was with the saints, you and I have been created by God for these days in which we live. Like them, he has created us for friendship with himself and with others, and like them he has created us for a mission. I pray that the stories of these great men and women and how they were transformed and sustained by the sacraments will rouse us to become saints ourselves in our day and age. May this cloud of witnesses, who even now cheer us on, inspire us to become ever more magnanimous, to desire to be great and to do great things—not for ourselves and our own glory, but for God and the good of those all around us who live the nightmare that is life without God.

Father John Riccardo

Authors' Note

The lives and backgrounds of the saints in this series were carefully researched. To depict key events of their lives in a dramatized way, we extrapolated from the research on each saint to provide details and dialogue that seemed likely.

The additional biographical information, along with the personal challenge and prayer, are intended as prompts that can inspire you to reflect in a deeper way on your call to holiness. The Reader's Guides, found at the end of the book, provide discussion questions and additional resources on the grace of the sacraments in the lives of each of these saints. These guides can be used for individual reflection or in a group.

The saints were ordinary human beings who, like ourselves, had gifts and shortcomings. They are saints because of how they responded to God's graced invitations: with extraordinary love. We hope that, through these stories, you will enjoy getting to know them as much as we did.

BAPTISM

Saint Paul

Apostle of Christ Crucified

BORN: ca. BC 6, Tarsus or Galilee

DIED: ca. AD 67, Rome

FEAST DAYS: January 25—Feast of the Conversion of Saint Paul; June 29—Feast of Saints Peter and Paul

PATRON: missionaries, evangelists, writers, tentmakers, rope makers, protection against hailstorms and snakes

The young Saul of Tarsus decisively strode through the temple precincts. Stephen, a vocal follower of the New Way, had just been brought before the Sanhedrin, and Saul didn't want to miss the confrontation. He needed to know more about this New Way, so he could understand its hold over the minds and hearts of the less educated.

"What right have they," he thought, "to replace our God-given Law with the ideas of some crazy rabbi who ended up crucified?" The scandal of it infuriated Saul. These people were tarnishing the messianic expectations with beliefs in a false messiah who, instead of establishing the Kingdom of God, had suffered the shameful death of crucifixion. Saul couldn't understand the appeal that devout Jews were finding in the teachings left by such a disreputable rabbi.

Originally from Tarsus, Saul had been drawn to Jerusalem by his desire to deepen his knowledge and love for the one true God. As a Pharisee, he had delighted in studying the Law and had dedicated his life to a close observance of the Law. Now Saul found the claims of Stephen's false messiah so disturbing that he even found himself at odds with his mentor, the revered and wise Rabbi Gamaliel. Gamaliel wanted to let the new movement die out on its own. Saul disagreed. Couldn't Gamaliel see how fast the errors were spreading? Some action should be taken!

Saul shouldered his way through the crowd, so he could hear and see everything. Stephen was forcefully making his case, quoting the Scriptures. He certainly was logical and eloquent, Saul admitted to himself. But then Stephen shouted, "I see the heavens open and the glory of God revealed, and the Son of Man on the right hand of the Father!"

Saul felt his gut clench at the blasphemy—Stephen was claiming that this rabbi Jesus was equal to God! He shouted out his indignation: "Blasphemy!"

Cries of "stone him!" filled the courtroom. The angry energy of the mob swept through Saul and even the Sanhedrin.

Some of the younger men took hold of Stephen and rushed him away to be stoned outside the Temple, which could not be defiled. Saul followed, fiercely glad that something was finally being done to stop these insults against God by those who claimed to believe in him.

When they arrived at the pit, the mob threw Stephen down into it. Everyone scrambled to pick up a rock, to take part in this purge of heresy. The doubts that Gamaliel had planted in Saul deterred him from hurling stones, but he showed his approval by watching over the cloaks of his companions.

He watched as Stephen fell to his knees and prayed aloud, "Lord, forgive them; they don't know what they're doing!" And Saul kept watching until the stones brought their target completely to the ground, and Stephen prayed aloud one last time, "Lord Jesus, receive my spirit!" That name again—Saul wanted to eradicate its haunting power from the earth. Yet as Stephen lapsed into stillness, something about the confident peace on his face disturbed the young Pharisee.

He pushed his misgivings aside as he returned his friends' cloaks. "These people are blasphemers, putting this Jesus at the side of God! We need to keep our momentum going. We need to destroy this New Way!"

Saul did not attempt to stone other followers of the New Way because only the Roman authorities had the legal authority to execute someone. Instead, he looked for ways to persecute the followers of Jesus—harassment, prison, physical punishment. For a while, it seemed to work. The name of Jesus was no longer spoken so openly in the Temple, and his followers scattered. Unwilling to see the New Way spread, Saul asked the elders for their unofficial approval to take his campaign against the New Way to nearby Damascus. He joined a caravan and set out on foot. After several days they drew close to Damascus. It was near noon, the sun's hot glare slowing even Saul's grim determination. He *knew* he was right in stopping the spread of the New Way, but for several nights Stephen's cries had been echoing through his dreams.

Suddenly, from out of nowhere, a burst of brilliant light stunned Saul. Eyes dazzled, he lost his balance and fell to the ground, peering up at the brilliance. A figure stood in the sky, at the center of the radiant light, but Saul couldn't make out any details. Then the figure drew closer, and Saul was able to distinguish the man's features. Dark, liquid eyes full of wise compassion penetrated deep inside him, past all his defenses. *Those eyes knew him, knew who he was, all he had done, all he longed to be.* It was a divine gaze, not of justice, but of love. Yet, a gaze tinged with sadness. Then, the light became so strong that Saul closed his eyes as the figure asked, "Saul . . . Saul . . . why are you persecuting me?"

Those words overwhelmed Saul. "Who . . . who are you, Lord?" he dared to ask.

"I am Jesus, whom you are persecuting."

He lay there stunned, feeling the world spinning around him. Gamaliel had warned him, yet he hadn't listened and had gotten everything wrong! *Jesus* was the *true* Messiah, the very Son of God! And he—Saul—had opposed him! For a moment, despair wrestled with Saul's memory of glimpsing that powerful gaze of love. Then, suddenly, he knew the one offer he could make.

He raised himself to a sitting position. "Lord, what do you want me to do?" he asked, looking up at the figure in the brightness.

"Get up and go into the city, where you will be told what to do," Jesus replied.

Then the sky darkened—so dark that Saul could see nothing at all. He stayed there, seated on the ground—stunned by the revelation he had received. He could hear the voices of the travelers near him, and finally, when one of them tried to lift him to his feet, Saul realized that the darkness of night had not fallen. He was blind! As he had been blind spiritually, now he was blind physically.

The soul-shattered Saul had to be led by the hand into the city of Damascus. His companions didn't understand what had happened. They hadn't seen Jesus, and they didn't know what to do with this broken man. They brought him to a place where he could lodge and left him there.

For three days, Saul struggled to understand his encounter with Christ on the road to Damascus. He couldn't eat or drink. His blindness was forcing him to think over what Jesus had revealed. The Law had been replaced by a Person—the Son of God. Saul's life as a persecutor was over. All that he had thought important was meaningless in the light of a God who had become man and had died to save all of humankind. Saul hadn't just made a mistake; his whole life was a mistake. Saul was a total failure.

Despair haunted Saul as the meaning of Jesus' words became clearer to him. "I am Jesus, whom you are persecuting." Every time he had harassed and imprisoned a follower of Jesus, he had chained and persecuted Jesus himself. Stephen's death—and his own part in it—would haunt him for the rest of his life. The only thing that gave Saul hope was his memory of glimpsing the face of the Lord Jesus. That penetrating, compassionate gaze would remain forever etched on the young Pharisee's heart.

On the third day, Saul's host interrupted his blind solitude to tell him that a man named Ananias was there to see him. Saul had had a dream about someone named Ananias the night before, but his ordeal had taken so much out of him that he was weak and trembling as he rose to greet his visitor.

Ananias laid his hands on Saul's head saying, "My brother Saul, the Lord Jesus who appeared to you has sent me to help you recover your sight and receive the Holy Spirit."

Saul felt something like scales fall from his eyes. He blinked in the dim light of the room—the first light he had seen in three days. An older man stood before him, cautiously waiting. In his desperate need, Saul reached out and grasped Ananias' hand, stiff with reserve. "You are his follower! Will Jesus ever forgive me? What am I supposed to do now so that the Lord will not abandon me?"

Ananias relaxed his stiff shoulders. "Jesus himself sent me to you. I think he has already forgiven you. He has chosen you to bring his name to both Gentiles and Jews. You know," Ananias added as he looked closely at Saul's gaunt face. "I didn't want to come here. I thought you'd do me harm. But the Lord insisted. He said that your mission will not be easy, and that you will suffer for his name."

A great weight lifted from Saul's chest. "What should I do?" he asked. "How can I begin to follow his Way? I have heard that you baptize new followers with water. Can I be baptized?"

Ananias released Saul's trembling hand. "Let's talk first. You may have questions about Jesus. And I think you need a good meal."

"*Then* will you baptize me?" Saul asked intensely.

Ananias smiled. "Gladly, once I am sure that you know what it means. For us, Baptism is more than just a purifying ritual. Jesus himself made the waters of Baptism holy when John the Baptist baptized him in the Jordan. Baptism in Jesus doesn't just take away sin. It's a new birth. We're born into a new life, the life that Jesus gives us, life in his Spirit."

Saul suddenly didn't know which of his many questions to ask, and he found it hard to stay on his feet. Ananias guided him to a seat, and during a meal he began instructing Saul.

Saul regained his strength, was baptized, and immediately sought to proclaim his newfound faith in Jesus, the crucified and risen Lord. Yet, all did not go smoothly. At first, Saul seemed better at stirring things up than living in harmony. The intensity of Saul's character and his unwavering, sometimes challenging approach to preaching the Gospel became a source of tension in the first Christian communities he lived in. Even when he went to Jerusalem to hear about Jesus from the apostles themselves, he stirred up resentment by his powerful preaching. Finally, the Church in Jerusalem sent him back to his home city of Tarsus.

For several years, Saul remained in Tarsus, earning a living by tentmaking while interiorizing and deepening the foundations of his faith and his relationship with the Lord Jesus.

Then Saul's friend Barnabas visited him and invited him to help minister to the Church in Antioch. After several months, at an assembly of prayer, the Holy Spirit spoke powerfully to the leaders of the Christians at Antioch, sending Barnabas and Saul as "apostles" to the Gentiles. This was the beginning of Saul's special mission as an apostle—a mission that lasted for the rest of his life. During his journeys throughout the Roman Empire, Saul used his Roman name—Paul. That is the name by which he is best known today.

It is estimated that Paul traveled tens of thousands of miles on foot and by sea as an apostle of his crucified Lord. Both the Acts of the Apostles and Paul's letters list the many sacrifices and dangers he faced, including imprisonment, stoning, shipwreck, and scourging as he sought to bring Christ's name everywhere. But Paul didn't care about his sufferings. His life had become so centered on Jesus that he would write, "For me, life *is* Christ." His biggest concern was for the churches that he had founded and visited, and he offered his sufferings, his "crucifixion with Christ," for their salvation and holiness. His warm affection for his communities and the intensity of his love for Christ nurtured the early Church. His letters express that warmth, his gratitude to his many close collaborators, and a "theology in action," for Paul was an innovative thinker as well as a decisive action-taker.

Finally, Paul was arrested during one of the Roman Emperor Nero's persecutions of the Christians. He was not afraid of death, knowing that nothing could separate him from Christ's love. Instead, he was grateful that he could offer himself completely to the One who had died for him. Worn out with a lifetime of service to the Gospel, Paul bowed his head under the sword of the executioner, finally sharing completely in the death and immortal life of his beloved Master.

Personal Challenge

When was the last time I sat in front of the Blessed Sacrament and allowed Jesus to look at me the way he gazed at Saint Paul?

Prayer

Saint Paul, your heart was filled to overflowing with the love of the Lord Jesus Christ. You fully lived your Baptism into his death and Resurrection, testifying to the world about Jesus not just with words and letters, but with your very life and death. May the love of Christ overflow into my life so that I, too, may witness to the unfathomable love of Christ to all whom I meet. May the fullness of Christ and the power of his love and purpose come to fruition in me so that I can say with you, "For me to live is Christ." Amen.

Notes on His Life

~::~ *How do we know so much about Saint Paul?* In the New Testament, we have his letters and the Acts of the Apostles. The Acts give us a valuable framework of Paul's life, but Paul's letters reveal the great heart and passion of the apostle.

~::~ *Did Saint Paul write all the* New Testament *letters attributed to him?* At the time the New Testament was being written, authorship was understood differently than it is today. In those days it was an accepted practice for writers to associate their works with famous persons to give more authority to their writing. Today's Scripture scholars do not agree about all the letters formerly attributed to Saint Paul. About half of these letters are accepted by all scholars as genuine (Romans, Galatians, 1 and 2 Corinthians, Philippians, 1 Thessalonians, and Philemon). Scholars who accept only those seven letters as written by Paul regard the other "Pauline" letters as written by his collaborators or other writers who summarized some of Paul's thoughts. Early Church tradition supports the Pauline authorship of all the letters. Scripture scholarship has its limits, and ongoing studies continue to reveal new information and insights. All thirteen letters are accepted as being "in the school" of Paul, and—most importantly—all are considered by the Church to be the inspired Word of God.

~::~ *How can one best describe Saint Paul, whose influence over the Church has been so great that some people erroneously call him the "founder" of Christianity?* Jesus Christ is the Founder of Christianity, but he entrusted much of the first outreach of his Church to Saint Paul, who became the missionary par excellence. Saint Paul was also a theologian, pastor, spiritual writer, and martyr. His letters sketch the earliest pictures we have of the Church and give us the language to describe spiritual and theological realities, such as Baptism and life in Christ. The best description of Paul himself comes from his own words: "apostle of Jesus Christ."

In His Own Words

> "God, who had set me apart before I was born and called me through his grace, was pleased to reveal his Son to me, so that I might proclaim him among the Gentiles."

Reader's Guide for Saint Paul, page 153.

Saint Cecilia

Singing God's Praises

Born: second or third century

Died: second or third century, martyr in Rome

Feast Day: November 22

Patron: music

With tears in her eyes, Cecilia looked down at the white tunic she was about to put on. It was perfect, woven of the finest linen, a fitting wedding garment for a young noblewoman of a wealthy Roman family. The young teenager's parents had arranged her marriage to Valerian, a nobleman in his early twenties. The few times they had met, Cecilia had been impressed by her groom's uprightness, his love for his brother Tiburtius, and his thoughtfulness. Romance had no place in arranged marriages in third century Rome, but Cecilia knew that her parents thought this marriage was best for her. The problem was that Cecilia didn't want to marry at all, and certainly not to someone who didn't share her beliefs, however noble he was!

An ardent Christian, Cecilia had tried to explain to her parents that following Jesus was the most important thing in the world to her. Even though it was risky to be a Christian—martyrdom was always a possibility—Cecilia had been able to practice her faith secretly for years, under her father's protection. Her parents were not believers, but up until now, they had tolerated Cecilia's adherence to the Christian faith. What they didn't understand was that years ago, in her desire to give herself completely to God, Cecilia had made a vow of virginity. She had promised God that she would remain a virgin forever and dedicate her entire life to him, sharing with others her belief in Jesus and serving Christ in those who were poor and needy. But her parents had never understood her beliefs, and now they were adamant that she marry Valerian.

What could she do? She had tried to explain her situation to her parents, at first together, and then separately. After two or three conversations, her father had forbidden her to speak on the topic again. When she protested, he had simply turned and walked away. Cecilia had hoped her mother would understand, but she too had insisted that Cecilia marry, completely dismissing her concerns. Her mother had pointed out that the handsome young man had a reputation for being kind and fair. He was a pagan, but Cecilia's mother thought that he might eventually allow Cecilia to live according to her beliefs; he seemed to be a good man who would probably tolerate Cecilia's strange ideas and habits as her parents had. Valerian's paganism might even keep her safe from the persecutions of the Christians that frequently flared up around the empire, making it dangerous even to gather for the Eucharist.

The priest that Cecilia had consulted about her situation had been sympathetic but had advised submission and prudence. Cecilia, however, felt that she couldn't tiptoe around Valerian forever. Was it even fair to marry him without telling him that she was a Christian and had made a vow of virginity that she meant to keep? How could she persuade Valerian to respect her vow? At some point, she'd have to trust Valerian and tell him. So why not tonight? Perhaps he wouldn't care she if she was a Christian. Perhaps he would convert. Or perhaps he would renounce her as his wife and turn her over to the emperor! These were dangerous times for Christians. Cecilia knew she'd be risking her life, but wasn't her life always in God's hands?

Cecilia's heart pounded within her as the servant came in to fix her hair. Cecilia couldn't see a way out of the wedding. She hadn't slept well the past three nights, praying and seeking the right words to confide her secret to Valerian. Despite her fears, Cecilia knew in her heart that to God, nothing was impossible. She would trust her true Bridegroom to come to her rescue, however he would choose to do so.

The servant finished her hair and helped her to dress. It was time!

The wedding ceremony and banquet seemed to drag on forever. Throughout the celebration, every time her fear arose, Cecilia renewed her trust. "My Jesus, my true Bridegroom, help me to be faithful to you!" Then the wedding feast was over. In candlelight procession, Cecilia and Valerian walked from the house where she had grown up to her new home. With all the noise of the celebration, they couldn't talk. But on the way, Cecilia caught Valerian watching her keenly.

At last, they arrived at Valerian's home, and Cecilia and Valerian were alone together.

Valerian held out his hand to his beautiful young bride. He seemed to be trying to put her at ease. Cecilia reached out and hesitantly took his hand, but before he could draw her closer, she forestalled him, her words rushing out.

"Valerian, I have to tell you something: an important secret about me. I beg of you to respect it!"

Valerian tensed. "Cecilia, I want to get to know you as my wife, and I will always respect you. Tell me what's been on your mind all day."

"I am a Christian," she blurted out, "and I have made a vow of virginity. I'm already promised to God." She held her breath. *He had noticed that she had been uneasy all day. What would he do?*

Valerian was stunned and confused. "You are a Christian? What do you mean you are promised to God?"

Cecilia's eyes lit up. He was giving her a chance to explain! "I believe that Jesus Christ is the Son of God, who came down from heaven to share our human life with us. He *died* to save us from sin and despair and suffering. I've been in love with him my whole life, and I promised him with a vow of virginity that I would dedicate my life to him completely. He is my real 'Bridegroom.'" She took a deep breath. "It's not that I don't respect you, Valerian. But I'm already promised."

Valerian hesitated. He seemed to be struggling to make sense of what she had said. He looked both hurt and confused. Then he spoke. "But how can you choose a God you cannot see, over a husband you can see?" he asked, trying to understand. "Are God's love and presence so real to you? More real than I am, standing here before you?" He took a step forward.

For a moment, Cecilia wanted to shrink back. Was he angry? She took a deep breath, then stepped closer to this man whose eyes were looking into hers for answers. She could see an undercurrent of something else in them—an emotion she couldn't quite identify.

"Yes, this Jesus is as real to me as you are. Just because I can't see him doesn't mean I don't sense his presence or see the way he works in my life. I hear the melody of his love every day, even though I cannot see his hands or the instrument he plays. He gives my life meaning, and he calls me to share in his work. He sends his angel to protect me. He walks beside me. I have nothing to fear from you because he is with me, right now."

As she spoke, Valerian's expression changed to wonder. "What is it like to be so sure of something that you would risk everything?" He took her by the hand and led her to a couch. "I am deeply moved. Tell me more," he urged. "Teach me about this God-Man whom you call Jesus Christ, and this angel who protects you."

Cecilia's face glowed with joy.

Over the next few months, Cecilia had the joy of sharing her faith not just with her new husband but with his brother Tiburtius as well. When the young men were baptized, Cecilia thought her heart would burst with happiness. Together, the three of them worked side by side to alleviate poverty and oppression in the city of Rome. The persecution of the Christians, spearheaded by Turcius Almachius, the Prefect of Rome, was growing fiercer by the day, and the trio found ways to secretly help the Christians who were suffering. They visited the imprisoned and buried the martyrs.

Cecilia's great joy was shaken when her husband and his brother were arrested as Christians. The prefect was especially eager to discredit noblemen who were sympathetic to the Christians, and Valerian and Tiburtius had become too well known for burying the Christian martyrs to be ignored. After their arrest, the two brothers were given an opportunity to offer incense to one of the gods of Rome. When they refused, they were executed by the sword. Maximus, the Roman official assigned to witness their execution, was so moved by their courageous faith that he, too, was converted and martyred shortly after.

Cecilia tearfully received their remains, rescued by other Christians, and buried them. She knew that despite their sufferings, they had joyfully offered their lives to God. However, she keenly felt the pain of loneliness and separation. She worried that she was not worthy to lay down her life for Christ, too.

Her fears proved groundless. Shortly after, Cecilia was accused of being a Christian. Brought before the prefect, Cecilia fearlessly affirmed her Christian faith and refused to sacrifice to the Roman idols. Fearing the consequences of the public execution of a noblewoman, Turcius Almachius ordered that she be suffocated to death in the steam bath of her own home. Soldiers heated the bath and locked her inside. Hours later, long after she should have died, they heard music. Opening the door, they found her miraculously alive and singing a hymn of praise to God.

The soldiers reported back to the prefect about what had happened. He then ordered that Cecilia be slain by the sword in her home. The executioner struck her neck three times, but either through nervousness or incompetence, he did not kill her outright. Instead, Cecilia was left there to suffer intensely for three days. As friends and spectators gathered around her, Cecilia, who was unable to speak, wanted to witness to her faith in God. With one hand, she held up one finger to express her faith in her one, beloved God. With the other hand, she raised three fingers to express her faith in the Trinity—Father, Son, and Holy Spirit, one God in Three Persons. With this simple gesture, Cecilia renewed her baptismal faith until her soul went forth to receive the inheritance of that faith—the loving embrace of the Father, Son, and Spirit to whom she had witnessed with her entire life.

Personal Challenge

Like Saint Cecilia, could my joyful witness of the faith be the turning point for someone to come to Christ?

Prayer

Saint Cecilia, the melody of God's love surrounded you and strengthened you in all your trials. You fearlessly lived your Baptism and offered your life as a witness to the triune love of God—Father, Son, and Spirit. Help us to hear and join in singing the melody of God's love to our world. Amen.

Notes on Her Life

~::~ Saints Cecilia, Valerian, and Tiburtius really existed and died as Christian martyrs sometime in the second or third centuries, when Christianity was illegal in the Roman Empire. Unknown numbers of followers of Jesus—whether in the thousands or the millions is still debated today—died as martyrs for their faith in Jesus. The stories and even the names of most of these early heroic witnesses have been lost.

The catacombs and early martyrologies give us the names of some, like Cecilia, Valerian, and Tiburtius. The details about Cecilia's life are reported in a fifth century text whose historical reliability is debated, the "Acts of the Martyrdom of Saint Cecilia."

~::~ By the fourth century, Saint Cecilia was being honored as a martyr; by the fifth century, she was one of the most venerated of the early martyrs. She is among the few saints whose name is included in the Canon of the Mass.

~::~ Saint Cecilia has been associated with music because of two legends about her: while the musicians played at her wedding, Cecilia sang to God in her heart, and, as the soldiers were trying to suffocate her, Cecilia sang the praises of God.

~::~ In the ninth century, Saint Cecilia appeared to Pope Paschal I, who was rebuilding Saint Cecilia's Church and searching for her remains to transfer them to the church. Saint Cecilia asked him to keep looking, telling him that he had gotten very close to her. Her remains were found and transferred, along with those of Valerian, Tiburtius, and Maximus.

~::~ Saint Cecilia was probably a wealthy woman because the Church of Saint Cecilia, built in the fourth century and dedicated to her in the fifth century, is thought to have been built on property Cecilia herself had donated to the Church. Excavations underneath the twice-restored church have uncovered Cecilia's third-century home, which can be toured today, including the bath where Cecilia was martyred.

In Her Own Words

"I am called Cecilia, but my most beautiful name is Christian."

Reader's Guide for Saint Cecilia, page 155.

CONFIRMATION

Saint Helena

The Holy Empress

Born: ca. 246–250, possibly at Drepanum in Bithynia, Asia Minor
Died: ca. 329, possibly at Constantinople (now Istanbul, Turkey)
Feast Day: August 18
Patron: archeologists, converts, difficult marriages, divorced persons
Recognized as a saint by the Catholic Church, Eastern Orthodox Churches, Oriental Orthodox Churches, and the Anglican and Lutheran Communions.

Helena paced the richly furnished room. She was tired from lack of sleep, the turmoil in her mind, and above all, the heartbreak. She had to stop mulling over what had happened: her anguished pleading with Constantine, the yearning in his eyes for her understanding and approval, her failure to prevent the executions. Those family tragedies had caused the first serious rift between her and her son. She'd always supported him unconditionally—this beloved son who had shared the painful time of her husband's desertion and had grown into such a fine and upright man. She felt that he was one of the greatest leaders the world had ever known. Helena knew that though Constantine held tremendous power, he tried to balance it with moderation, prudence, and justice. As emperor and the most powerful man in the world, her son had to act in the best interest of the empire. But he was human, and the pull of emotion could unbalance the best of judgments—even an emperor's.

Could she have prevented the deaths of her favorite grandson, Crispus, and her daughter-in-law? Yet, betrayals had consequences, and she couldn't change the past.

"What can I do," she mused to herself. "Something to heal our family, to bring our focus back to living for Christ and serving the Church." Suddenly her eyes brightened. She knew exactly what she wanted to do.

That night at supper, Helena dined alone with her son as she had requested. Though lately Helena felt her age more, the resemblance between mother and son was still perceptible; they shared the same energetic determination and the same upright bearing. But Constantine had his father's fiery eyes and dark, curly hair. His manner was a bit stiff now, their recent sorrows and disagreements lingering.

"Son, I have an idea." Helena broke the silence casually. "I hope you won't object."

Emperor Constantine looked at his mother uneasily. Then as he saw her smile, he relaxed. "I know I will object, Mother. Your ideas are often . . . startling, shall we say?"

"Unexpected is more precise." Helena's smile was so quick that her son almost missed it. "It's been safe for some time to travel across the empire, hasn't it? I want you to arrange a trip for me . . . to Jerusalem." She tried to sound casual, knowing that she was indeed proposing something—as he had said—*startling*.

"What!?" Constantine looked at his seventy-five-year-old mother in disbelief.

"I want to follow in the footsteps of Christ, to go to the actual places where our Savior, the Lord Jesus Christ himself, walked, preached, suffered, and died. It will be a pilgrimage to thank God for his goodness and to ask his blessing on our family and on the empire. And I want to build churches fit to honor those holiest of places. The world today needs to remember the center and core of Christianity—that a humble, self-emptying son of a carpenter died on a cross to save us. Christians must not forget that *he* gives suffering new meaning."

"But you're—" Constantine swallowed the tactless words. Such a journey would be a great sacrifice, even considering the comforts with which a mother-empress would be provided. Such a pilgrimage would separate them, perhaps for years. But Constantine could see that she had made her decision. If he did not arrange the trip, she would find a way to go on her own. He made one last try.

"It's a brilliant idea. But such a journey will be long and difficult. What if we send a team of architects, and they . . ."

Helena laid her hand on her son's arm. "I want to go myself. This is a pilgrimage I will make for us, for our family."

Constantine looked in her eyes and knew he could not refuse her—not again. "I must be crazy," Constantine muttered, "but I'll do it . . . . I'll arrange the trip. You must promise to return safely." When he saw her smile, he knew that somehow this pilgrimage would make things right between them.

On her journey, Helena practiced the charity for which she had become so well known in Rome: providing for hungry and poor people in the villages through which her entourage passed.

Meanwhile, the solitude of traveling only with servants gave her plenty of time to pray and reflect on the journey of her life.

Helena had been the daughter of an innkeeper—a humble beginning for a life that would become intertwined with the lives of leaders of the Roman Empire. When in her early twenties, she had met Captain Flavius Julius Constantius (nicknamed Chlorus because of his pale complexion). They had fallen in love and married. Their son, Constantine, had become Helena's close companion while his father traveled on campaign, soon rising to the rank of general. Whenever Constantius Chlorus returned, he would relive his military adventures with Helena. Her keen mind was able to grasp his battle tactics and enjoy his stories. And he had loved her for it. Helena hadn't complained about his long absences, but she'd missed him intensely when he was gone.

As Helena continued to recall the events of her past, the painful part came to life before her eyes:

One day, after a particularly joyful reunion with his family, Constantius received a letter from the Emperor Maximian, summoning him to Rome. He was to leave as soon as possible. That evening Constantius and Helena went out into the warm night air and talked for hours. The boat was to sail the next day. Time was short, so terribly short.

"You tell Constantine this time," Constantius said huskily. "I can't."

"I'll tell him," Helena replied. "Don't look so glum, Constantius; this is good news! Once you find out your new appointment, you'll return to us. It won't take long . . . and we'll be waiting here, Constantine and I."

Months passed—longer than Helena had anticipated. Finally, a messenger from the emperor arrived. He seemed uneasy when he entered the room, and Helena, expecting Constantius rather than a messenger, immediately stood up.

"What is it?"

"I have a message for you," he stammered. "The Emperor Maximian has appointed Constantius his 'Caesar' to assist him in governing the western part of the Empire—Britain, Gaul, and Spain."

Helena's fear changed to joy, though a part of her mind noted that it was odd that the messenger remained so reluctant and uneasy. "When can I expect Constantius to arrive home?" Her mounting excitement turned to perplexity as the messenger hesitated again.

"He isn't coming alone," he mumbled. "The emperor insisted that, in keeping with his new position, General Constantius had to marry the emperor's stepdaughter, Theodora. One does not say 'no' to the emperor. The divorce has already taken place. Constantius and Theodora are already married." He mumbled his last words. "They'll arrive here in less than two months."

"I must go away," she said, too stunned to say anything else.

"And Constantine must await him here—it's his father's orders," the messenger added.

"I must go *alone*," she murmured brokenly.

How long had it taken for the emptiness in her heart to become bearable? Helena herself did not know. She had spent the next fifteen years quietly, following from afar the affairs of the new Caesar and those of her son, who was also rising politically. In 305, Constantius Chlorus became Caesar Augustus—Emperor of the West. He immediately called Constantine to his side to inherit his title. When Constantius died only a year later, Constantine was acclaimed Caesar Augustus by his father's soldiers. But other claimants vied for the imperial throne. Constantine waged one battle after another until he met his biggest rival, Maxentius, who had troops greatly outnumbering his own. The day before battle, Constantine saw a brilliant light in the sky, shaped like a cross. A voice told him, "By this sign you shall conquer." It was the sign of the God of the Christians. The following day, at the Milvian Bridge outside Rome, Constantine won a complete victory. And the new Caesar Augustus became fascinated by Christianity.

For three hundred years, Christians had suffered scorn, misunderstanding, contempt, and barbarous persecution . . . and their religion had not only survived, but grown. The Christ of Galilee held a deep fascination for those seeking truth, meaning, and an upright way of life. Finally, the Master's love touched the emperor himself. Constantine published the Edict of Milan, not only freeing Christians from persecution, but also ensuring their legal rights and the return of their property seized in persecution.

Having secured the western empire at last, Constantine invited Helena to join him at Rome, treating her with the same affection that he'd always had for her. Her lonely exile was finally over!

Helena was happy to be reunited with her son, but even the honors he wanted to pour upon her couldn't heal her heart from the desertion and sense of loss she had suffered all those years ago. At first, she was curious about her son's enthusiasm for Christianity, but then she became intrigued. She found something captivating in stories about Jesus, who taught humility, purity, the dignity of every person, and love of one's neighbor as testimony to love for God. Even more than that, Helena wondered about Jesus' suffering and death, in which the recent

Christian martyrs so gladly shared. Was it possible that Jesus could do what no one else could—heal her broken heart and give meaning to all her pain and suffering?

Helena was baptized a Christian at the age of sixty-three, and the city of Rome quickly fell in love with the impetuous, gracious lady. Constantine showered extraordinary honors and privileges on her, even placing the treasury of the empire at her disposal. The empress mother dipped into it to give alms, not just from a distance, but personally to the people of Rome who were poor, sick, enslaved, or occupied in hazardous work, such as the soldiers and miners. She also used funds from the treasury to build magnificent churches in Rome. Helena focused on doing good and avoided politics, apart from supporting her son. Constantine was extraordinarily capable, even reuniting East and West into one empire.

But then the worst crisis of all had come. After reuniting the entire empire, Constantine discovered betrayals within his own family and had had both his firstborn son and wife executed. Heartbroken, Helena especially feared the harm this rift might have done to her son. This pilgrimage was as much for him as for her.

Finally arriving in the Holy Land, Helena herself directed efforts to find and restore the holy sites. She took great comfort walking in the footsteps of Jesus. Perhaps she didn't realize how closely she was following the crucified Master—she carried her sorrows with her to Jerusalem. There she finally found peace, uniting her sufferings to those of Christ on the Cross.

With the cooperation of Bishop Macarius of Jerusalem, she restored holy sites, building at least two magnificent churches. She continued to give of herself to those in need, often serving the poor with her own hands. After several years in the Holy Land, Helena started her return journey, but she traveled slowly, building churches or providing for their construction wherever needed.

The frail mother empress finally rejoined her son, but she had greatly aged. She died in the year 330, with Constantine at her side. Helena joyfully went to meet her crucified Lord, who had filled the emptiness in her life with overflowing peace.

Personal Challenge

Like Saint Helena, can I allow the Holy Spirit to renew me no matter what age I am?

Prayer

Saint Helena, you came to know Christ late in your life, yet you decisively embraced the Christian faith, allowing the Holy Spirit to lead you to follow in the footsteps of Jesus. You discovered how to unite your sufferings to Jesus on the cross. Grant me a deep appreciation for the mysteries of the suffering, death, and Resurrection of Jesus. Help me to become as you were: a fearless witness to Christ in the world throughout my daily life. Amen.

Notes on Her Life

~::~ We know little of Helena's life until her sixties. We don't know how or where Helena met Constantius. His divorcing her for political purposes was not unusual at the time.

- ~::~ Before the Edict of Milan, both Constantius Chlorus and Constantine were kindly disposed toward Christians and avoided persecuting them.
- ~::~ While some legends speak of Helena converting Constantine, earlier sources affirm that Constantine introduced his mother to Christianity, who embraced it more enthusiastically than her son. Constantine grew in his faith throughout his life and was baptized shortly before his death.
- ~::~ It is not known why Constantine executed his own son Crispus and his wife, Fausta. One source indicates that Helena may have indirectly caused Fausta's death because she told Constantine that Fausta had falsely accused Crispus.
- ~::~ The true cross was discovered during the Emperor Constantine's reign. About sixty years after Saint Helena's death, two sources name her as the discoverer of the true cross. This is one of the reasons why she is especially remembered on September 14, the Feast of the Triumph of the Cross. On the other hand, it is possible that Helena gave her son the idea of searching for the true cross.
- ~::~ Whether Saint Helena or her son discovered the true cross, it is certain that Saint Helena's personal devotion led her to visit the Holy Land and restore several sacred sites and build at least two churches: the Church of the Nativity in Bethlehem and the Church of the Ascension on the Mount of Olives.

Helena's Devotion to the Cross As Expressed by Saint Paul

> "May I never boast of anything except the cross of our Lord Jesus Christ, by which the world has been crucified to me, and I to the world."

Reader's Guide for Saint Helena, page 157.

Saint Lorenzo Ruiz

"Accidental" Martyr

Born: ca. 1610, Binondo, Manila, Philippines

Died: September 1637, Nagasaki, Japan

Feast Day: September 28

Patron: the Philippines, Filipino and Chinese youth

Lorenzo's heart hammered so hard he thought it would push through his chest. *That would put an end to my terror,* he thought irrationally. He tried to turn away from the horror of the water torture Father Antonio was enduring, but the Japanese soldier at his side forced Lorenzo to turn back.

His panicked gaze met Father Antonio's. Pain gripped the priest's face, yet all he could do was grunt in agony after the water had been forced out of him. Was this the fourth or fifth time they had put the tall, frail priest through this inhuman torture? A year in prison hadn't improved any of the prisoners' health, but Father Antonio, the superior of their mission, had weakened most. He wouldn't survive much longer.

And then it would be Lorenzo's turn. They hadn't bothered to question him, simply assumed that Father Antonio spoke for him as well. *I am neither a priest nor a missionary! I didn't want to come here! I was not planning to convert anybody. I was just trying to avoid being executed. I don't want to die like this!*

Another companion, Lazaro—a layman like himself—huddled in a corner, unable to watch. He had already said that he would renounce his faith to save his own life. Lorenzo desperately wanted to join him, despite the shame. Physical terror made every nerve in his body scream for him to flee. *What can I do?*

Looking around, Lorenzo beckoned to one of the translators, a Portuguese man named Carvalho. As Lorenzo waited for him to come closer, his soul twisted with a combination self-loathing and fear. But he couldn't help himself. He had to know. *Was there a way out of this?*

"I want to speak to you privately," Lorenzo said. Carvalho waited impassively. Lorenzo took a deep breath, and over the pounding of his heart, whispered the terrible question. "If I apostatize, can my life be spared?" He looked down, hating the cowardice that prompted him even to ask such a question. Finally, he glanced up to see Carvalho studying him.

"You'll have to ask the judges," Carvalho said, no pity in his voice. A soldier called him away, and without a backward glance, Carvalho walked out of the room. The terrible weight of fear, and the choice being forced upon him, pressed Lorenzo so heavily that he backed up against the wall.

Lorenzo had been preparing himself for this moment since they had first been captured a little over a year ago. But witnessing Father Antonio's torture horrified him past reason, past anything! How could he not give in to the demands of the government officials that he renounce his faith, his Church, his God? What good would he do by choosing death? His wife and children would never know why he hadn't come back to them; they would never even know he'd died. Surely, it would be better to pretend to renounce Christianity and stay alive. Didn't he have a duty to his family?

The pounding in Lorenzo's heart eased slightly. Staying alive was all he wanted. There was nothing wrong with that.

Then Lorenzo looked back at Father Antonio, lying stripped and helpless on the ground, and his heart broke. *I'm not brave enough to suffer and die for Christ, but am I really capable of such a betrayal? They are my brothers . . . Christ is my Brother!*

Until recently, Lorenzo would never have questioned himself or God. He had been born in Binondo, a village in the Philippines designed to keep Chinese Christians outside the wall that the conquering Spaniards had built around Manila. His father was Chinese, his mother Filipino. Lorenzo had been raised as a Catholic and served as an altar boy and later, as a member of the Holy Rosary Confraternity. Educated at the Dominican schools, Lorenzo took on the profession of a scribe, writing out official documents by hand. This was a much-needed service since the majority of the population couldn't read or write.

Lorenzo had been blessed not just with a good trade, but also with a beautiful wife and three children—two sons and a daughter. How much he missed his family now! But there was no way to go back. He had been accused of involvement in the murder of a Spaniard. As a mestizo—son of both the conquered Filipino people and the suspect Chinese—Lorenzo had feared an unfair trial from the Spanish authorities. Certain that he would be convicted and hanged, he'd felt his only chance to avoid execution was to flee from any place where the Spaniards could find him.

The superior of the Dominicans, Father Domingo Gonzalez, had offered him the opportunity to board a ship secretly leaving the Philippines. Lorenzo had been so grateful for an escape that he had not pressed for information about the ship's secret destination. Only after they embarked had he learned that he had joined a secret missionary expedition to Japan, where Christianity was not only illegal, but Christians were actively persecuted. They were making no stops on the way where it would be safe for Lorenzo to disembark—all nearby territories were occupied by Spaniards who could be on the watch to capture him. Thus, although escaping trial and almost certain death by hanging, Lorenzo had found himself facing a future almost equally bleak.

His companions on this clandestine mission had been more aware of the dangers they faced, but even they were surprised by the quick action of the Japanese officials. Within a week of their arrival in Okinawa, they had been picked up and imprisoned on suspicion of being Christian. They had languished in prison for over a year, where Lorenzo had grown close to his companions.

Tall and gentle, Dominican Father Antonio Gonzalez was the group's superior. Father Guillaume Courtet, French, was in his mid-40s; Father Miguel de Aozaraza, a few years younger, was from Spain. Both were Dominican priests who had volunteered for this mission. Father Vincente Shiwozuka de la Cruz was a Japanese priest who had volunteered to guide them in Japan. During the brief voyage, he had joined the Dominicans and taken his vows. Lazaro Kyoto, the other layman in the group, was also Japanese. He had been expelled from Japan for being a leper, but had risked returning so he could help guide the missionaries to the persecuted Catholics in Japan.

A few days ago they had been split into two groups, with Fathers Guillaume, Miguel and Vincente taken to Nagasaki ahead of them. Just this morning Lorenzo, Lazaro, and Father Antonio had arrived here in Nagasaki, and Lorenzo had caught a glimpse of the infamous Nishazaka Hill where thousands of Japanese Catholic martyrs had died, witnessing to their faith in Jesus.

Immediately, they had been taken before several judges, who told them that their other companions had already renounced their faith. Lorenzo suspected that the judges were just trying to put more pressure on them, but Lazaro had immediately given in to the threats. He said he would reject his faith if his life was spared. The judges had been pleased and Lazaro relieved. But he had been kept there to witness Father Antonio's terrible torture.

Now, the soldiers dragged a collapsed Father Antonio away. Lorenzo waited for them to seize him, but instead, they forced Lazaro into position, telling him bluntly that he would not be spared the terrible torture because they wanted any information he might have. Lorenzo shuddered at Lazaro's screams.

Lord Jesus, Lorenzo prayed. *I'm weak and afraid. Free me from my fear. I still don't understand why you have brought me here, but give me the strength to choose to stand witness to you, to proclaim you not only through my life, but also through my death, if that's what you will.* Lorenzo's heart was still pounding, but a sudden deep conviction filled his heart with peace. He was no longer torn by indecision.

The soldiers finally believed Lazaro's babbling and took him to the next room to question him. Just as they turned to take

Lorenzo, Carvalho returned. Without allowing Carvalho to speak, Lorenzo said, "What I asked you before, I said without knowing what I was saying. I am a Christian, and I profess it until the hour of my death. For God I shall give my life." Then he added, "I didn't come to Japan to be a martyr but because I could not stay in Manila. But as a Christian and for God I shall give my life."

Carvalho watched as the soldiers forced Lorenzo to undergo the same torture as Father Antonio. They repeated the agonizing procedure time after time. During a break, a guard stood over Lorenzo and looked down on him—naked, soaked, and seizing up with pain. "Renounce your faith, and we'll stop! You can save yourself from all of this if you apostatize!" Lorenzo did not have the strength to speak but slowly shook his head. They propped him up and began again.

Finally, they dragged Lorenzo to a prison cell near Father Antonio and Lazaro. Separated only by thin walls of wood, they could speak to each other. The other three priests were also imprisoned there. All of them suffered terribly—the three priests who had arrived first had already endured several days of torture. They were too weak to stand and could barely speak, but they encouraged each other through the long night and following day. The other prisoners, the guards, and the translators caught parts of their conversations and were amazed at their courage and joy—they even teased one another wryly about their sufferings. That night, Lorenzo pondered in a new light the meaning of the sacred words he'd so often heard: "I live by faith in the Son of God, who loved me and gave himself for me" (Gal 2:20).

A day later, Father Antonio, Lazaro, and Lorenzo were tortured again. Father Antonio was soon sent back to his cell because of his weakened state. Lorenzo was brought to speak before the judges one last time. If he had any desire to escape torture and death, this was his chance. But the grace of God had transformed Lorenzo from a fearful runaway to a defiant witness. They pressed him. "If we grant you life, will you renounce your faith?"

Without any hesitation, Lorenzo answered, "Never! I am a Christian, and I shall die for God. For him, I would give a thousand lives if I had them. Do with me as you please."

Lorenzo's complete commitment of his life to God did not ease the physical pain he underwent, but it did give him the strength to endure. That night, Father Antonio died. Lazaro, who had once again been tortured and imprisoned with them, begged for forgiveness from his companions. They gave it gladly.

The rest of the week passed in a blur of suffering, except for Lazaro's public renewal of his own profession of faith. Not one of them wavered again, despite their severe sufferings.

On September 27, 1537, the five men were publicly paraded on horseback to Nishazaka Hill, gagged so they couldn't preach. Five gallows had been raised with five pits dug beneath them. Each was hanged upside down from the gallows, face just above the foul bottom of the pit. This excruciating form of execution could last for many days, but the authorities decided to hurry their deaths. On September 29, they were taken down. The three priests were found to be still alive and were beheaded. Lorenzo and Lazaro had already entered eternity.

At the supreme moment of crisis, the grace of God had transformed the seemingly unremarkable Lorenzo Ruiz into a heroic witness who freely offered his life for Christ.

Personal Challenge

Like Saint Lorenzo, who was faced with a painful and unwanted situation, can I allow the Holy Spirit to work through my trials and transform them into something unexpectedly beautiful?

Prayer

Saint Lorenzo, you were an ordinary husband and father whose life seemed unremarkable. But at your moment of truth, the graces God had showered on you throughout your life bore fruit. Instead of giving in to fear, you generously offered your life to God a thousand times over. Obtain for us the spirit of faith to recognize there are no "accidents" with God. Like you, may we discover the love God offers to us in our ordinary lives and in the sacraments so that, freed from fear, we can witness at every moment to Christ's love for us and for every person. Amen.

Notes on His Life

~::~ We know so little about Lorenzo because most of his life was so ordinary. The few facts we do know come from the eyewitness accounts of his trial and death, or from the testimony of the Dominicans who knew him in Manila.

~::~ Lorenzo's fidelity to his faith is all the more astonishing because he did not seek to be a missionary or a martyr; he was simply running from trouble.

~::~ The kinds of extreme torture that Lorenzo and his companions underwent were so horrible that simply the threat of them caused many Catholics to renounce their faith. Two translators present at their trial and torture—Antonio Carvalho and Pedro Rodrigues—were so impressed with each martyr's courage and faith that they secretly wrote eyewitness accounts and smuggled them out of Japan.

- One of the translators at Lorenzo's trial was the Jesuit priest Cristobal Ferreira, who had renounced his faith several years earlier after lengthy torture. Almost twenty years later, Father Ferreira publicly reclaimed his faith and underwent extreme torture again, this time dying as a martyr.
- Within three months of Lorenzo's death, the Dominican priests in Manila and Lorenzo's family found out about the martyrdom of the five companions.
- Lorenzo Ruiz is the first canonized Filipino saint.

His Last Words

"I am a Christian, and I shall die for God. For him, I would give a thousand lives if I had them."

Reader's Guide for Saint Lorenzo Ruiz, page 159.

EUCHARIST

Saint Thomas Aquinas

Humble Giant

BORN: ca. 1225, at his family's castle Roccasecca, near Aquino in what is now Italy

DIED: March 7, 1274, Fossanova, Italian peninsula

FEAST DAY: January 28

DECLARED DOCTOR OF THE CHURCH: 1567, by Pope Pius V

PATRON: students, schools and universities, thunderstorms

The solid, well-built man with slightly balding head and gentle eyes sighed as he put down his quill and stood to his full, imposing height. He looked down at the parchment he had finished. Thomas Aquinas was one of the most respected and acclaimed scholars of his day. Yet his was a humble genius, and today he was troubled. The prestigious University of Paris had asked him to answer a scholarly question about the mystery of the Eucharist, a question that divided students and faculty. The peaceful Thomas was deeply moved in prayer and meditation but rarely by the conflict and upheaval surrounding him—whether political or academic. Yet, now he was troubled by strong feelings of inadequacy! He was profoundly aware that, despite his years of study and gifts of intellect, he could never really understand the divine mystery of the Eucharist. Had he done justice to the question? How could he write worthily of Jesus' presence in the Most Holy Eucharist? He knew only one way to resolve his inner turmoil.

Decisively, he picked up the parchment and took it to the chapel. There, Thomas laid it at the foot of the crucifix and went to his usual place of prayer. He always offered his studies and teachings to the Divine Master, but today, he offered his writing with a special intensity. "Lord Jesus Christ, I humbly beg of you, if what I have written of this most holy Mystery is true, say so. But if it is not, please stop me from going further."

As Thomas fell deeper into adoration, he didn't notice Friar Reginald enter the chapel. Reginald was Thomas' confrere, companion, confessor, and collaborator. He knew that Thomas was troubled by the university's request. Thomas Aquinas had one of the finest minds the Church would ever have, but he was also the humblest man Reginald had ever known. How had the second cousin of the emperor, raised in privilege and academia, remained so humble? Reginald reflected on what he knew about Thomas.

This son of Count Landulf and Countess Theodora of Aquino, had been sent as a child to study with the monks at Montecassino, a nearby Benedictine monastery. His family had thought that one day Thomas might become a Benedictine monk and the abbot of that great and important monastery, wielding not just spiritual authority but political power as well. The monks must have recognized Thomas' great intellect because they recommended to his father that he continue his studies at the university. At fourteen, Thomas began studying at the University of Naples, but unlike many of the other students, Thomas continued to live a simple, devout life. In Naples he eventually met the Dominicans and felt drawn to enter their order. However, they counselled him to wait because they suspected that he'd have to face great resistance from his family. The family might consider it a disgrace for a nobleman of Thomas' status to enter such a humble order.

For three years Thomas waited, continuing his studies and nurturing his vocation. At age nineteen, he finally entered the Dominican order and was overjoyed to receive the rough white woolen tunic and black cloak that distinguished the followers of Dominic. His family, however, was dismayed at the news. His mother sent two of Thomas' brothers to waylay him and bring him back to the family's castle. There, they forcibly removed his treasured religious habit and imprisoned him for more than a year, trying to convince him to leave the Dominicans.

Thomas, however, proved true to his vocation. Despite the isolation, physical hardships, and unrelenting pressure from his entire family, he was unruffled—except when his brothers stooped to the low tactic of bringing in a prostitute to tempt him against chastity. Thomas picked up a burning brand from the fireplace and chased her out. Gradually, he persuaded several family members to take his side. His imprisonment grew easier when his sisters started smuggling books to him, and Thomas could continue his theological and philosophical studies as if he were at the university. At last his family caved in—whether because of Thomas' stubbornness or pressure from the Church—and allowed him to escape. Thomas was lowered from his prison tower in a huge basket.

Friar Reginald smiled to himself as he tried to picture the

solidly-built Thomas crammed into a basket, no matter what the size. How eagerly the Dominicans had welcomed Thomas back! But even after Thomas made his vows, influential family members had continued to insist that the young man leave the Dominicans. Thomas, however, remained firm in his conviction that he was where God had called him.

The young friar then began his studies under the great Dominican teacher Albert the Great. Although Thomas advanced quickly, outpacing the other students, he continued to be so quiet that he gained not only the reputation of being stupid but also the nickname, "dumb ox."

Albert didn't immediately recognize the treasure studying under him until a student slipped him some of Thomas' notes. The next day, Albert gave Thomas a rigorous oral test in front of the class, attacking his arguments from every possible angle. At the end, marveling at Thomas' responses, he said publicly to the class, "I tell you, the bellowing of this 'ox' will be heard around the world." After that, Albert took Thomas aside to tutor him personally. He also pressed Thomas to start teaching the other students and to speak up in class. The other students quickly discovered that Thomas' summaries were not only shorter, but often better thought out and more easily understood than the lessons of their teachers.

At the Dominican friary, Thomas stood out as much for his simple, unaffected humility as for his intellectual gifts. He clearly put others ahead of himself and carried his convictions into both actions and attitudes. Although he counseled popes and kings, he remained a humble and obedient friar. Once when Thomas was visiting another friary, a friar who didn't know who he was told him to come with him to do some errands—that the superior had said to take as a companion "the first friar he found." Rather than objecting that he was busy or explaining who he was, Thomas accompanied the friar on the errands. Later, the other friar was deeply embarrassed, but for Thomas it had simply been a matter of obeying the superior and assisting a confrere.

Of all the friars in the monastery, it was Reginald who knew the most about Thomas' impressive scholastic achievements and writings. Thomas not only carried out the role of teacher at the university—demanding in itself—but was usually writing and working on several other projects as well. He was in the middle of the greatest synthesis of the Catholic faith ever written, his *Summa Theologiae,* and he eagerly listened to the questions of the day so he could respond to them. In addition, Thomas was frequently recruited as a consultant by the great men of his time—the pope, King Louis IX, and other scholars.

And yet, Reginald mused, here Thomas was, wondering if he was worthy to write about the Eucharist. Reginald shook himself, clearing his head of the distracting riddle of his friend's character so he could pray. Suddenly, he heard a voice. Looking up, he saw a vision of Jesus standing on the manuscript that Thomas had placed at the foot of the crucifix. He heard Jesus say to Thomas, "You have written well of the sacrament of my Body."

Thomas' absorption in prayer deepened, and his body slowly levitated—lifting several feet from the ground. Reginald glanced at the other friars praying in the chapel. From their bewildered expressions, he knew that they were seeing what he was.

Reginald had suspected that Thomas had been graced with extraordinary experiences in prayer, but he was astonished to witness one. Some time later, Thomas sank gradually to the ground. Eventually he finished praying, and, as if nothing had happened, walked over to the crucifix and picked up the parchment. Reginald followed him out of the chapel. Thomas was often a bit preoccupied, but today he quickly became aware of Reginald's footsteps.

Thomas turned back and held out the parchment. "Doubts resolved?" Reginald probed. Thomas paused and searched his face. His curiosity changed to dismay as he read Reginald's expression.

"Please," he begged Reginald, "don't tell anyone."

Reginald nodded. "A couple of other friars were there. I don't think they'll keep quiet, even if I ask them to. But, Thomas, aren't you happy?"

"I'm at peace," Thomas admitted. "Now I can focus my attention on other concerns."

"But Jesus *said*—"

"It's all grace, Reginald. It's all gift. Everything I do—it's because God has blessed me. There's no special merit in it. I am happy and relieved that I've been useful."

"Useful!" sputtered Reginald. But Thomas smiled and hurried off, leaving Reginald behind holding the precious parchment.

Thomas continued to tirelessly respond to the needs of the Church and of his beloved Dominican Order. His entire life was spent praying, teaching, preaching, and writing. He frequently traveled to settle difficult questions or disputes among scholars. A close adviser to several popes, he served at the papal Curia, as well as in universities all over Europe, including Naples, Paris, Cologne, and Bologna. When Pope Clement IV tried to appoint him archbishop of Naples in 1265, Thomas begged to be excused, desiring always to remain a humble

Dominican friar and continue to dedicate his energies to wrestling with the great questions of Faith.

His preaching regularly drew large crowds, for his homilies were known to be simple, lucid, and eloquent. He devoted all his energies to seeking to understand and explain always better the Catholic faith.

One day after Thomas had completed the section of the *Summa Theologiae* on the Eucharist, Jesus spoke to him again in prayer. "You have written well of me, Thomas; what reward can I give you?" Thomas answered, "Yourself, O Lord; nothing but yourself!"

Thomas' untiring service gradually took its toll on his health. Then, on December 6, 1273, Thomas had a profound, life-changing experience in prayer. He never revealed what happened, but he stopped writing—something he had never done before. Concerned about him, some of the other friars urged Reginald to approach Thomas. Reginald hesitated a few days, then encouraged Thomas to continue his writing. Thomas told him simply, "I can't." Reginald pressed him. "But you haven't finished your *Summa Theologiae*! Your work is for God's glory and the world's . . . ."

Thomas interrupted him. "I can do no more. Such secrets have been revealed to me that all I have written and taught seem to be just a handful of straw." He never offered any further explanation, but began preparing for death.

In the early spring of 1274, Pope Gregory X summoned him to the general council at Lyons, and despite his great fatigue, Thomas set out for Lyons. He never made it. On the way, he suffered a head injury in an accident, which may have caused a blood clot in his brain. He stopped at the house of his niece; then, realizing that he was dying, he sought shelter in the nearby Cistercian abbey of Fossanova.

Even though he knew he was dying, Thomas honored the request of the monks to comment on the Song of Songs from his bed. Finally, he had no strength to continue. He asked Reginald to hear his confession and give him Viaticum. At dawn, while praying aloud one of his hymns to Jesus in the Eucharist, Thomas surrendered his soul to God. The date was March 7, 1274.

Thomas had finally received the reward he had asked for: "Nothing but yourself, Lord."

Personal Challenge

In the spirit of Saint Thomas Aquinas who often knelt before Jesus, asking the Lord's guidance and blessing upon his work, set aside some time to pray before Jesus present in the Blessed Sacrament.

Prayer

Saint Thomas, you humbly remained true to your vocation to preach the Gospel through family opposition, imprisonment, and misguided admiration. Your fidelity bore fruit in your prayer and your writings. Your reasoned and faith-filled approach to philosophy and theology still guides the Church today. Share with us your own gratitude for the Eucharistic Mystery: a sacred banquet in which we receive Christ himself, renew our memory of his suffering and dying for us, and rejoice in the promise of future glory of everlasting union with God, which you now enjoy. Amen.

Notes on His Life

~::~ While he was imprisoned by his family, who were trying to prevent him from becoming a Dominican, Thomas influenced at least two of his siblings: his worldly sister Marotta became a cloistered nun and eventually abbess of her community; his married sister Theodora, a countess, became known for her holiness. Thomas later wrote about the importance of a young person's freedom to follow his or her vocation to religious life.

~::~ When asked what was the greatest grace he had received, Thomas said that it was to have understood every page he ever read.

~::~ Thomas' early mentor, often referred to as Saint Albert the Great, became his close collaborator and friend throughout his life.

~::~ Thomas was not a boring or isolated academic; he used new resources and an innovative style of teaching and writing to brilliantly address the questions of his day with accuracy, brevity, and completeness. He taught that the true relationship between faith and reason is not one of opposition, but natural harmony. One of his great accomplishments was to systematize theology.

~::~ Thomas dictated most of his works, sometimes to four secretaries simultaneously. Today his writings fill more than twenty volumes.

~::~ He wrote beautiful eucharistic prayers and hymns that are still used today (such as the *Tantum Ergo*).

~::~ At the Council of Trent, the council fathers used only three books for reference: the Bible, the decrees of the popes, and Thomas' *Summa Theologiae*. If Thomas had accepted Pope Clement IV's appointment as archbishop of Naples, we probably wouldn't have the *Summa Theologiae* today.

In His Own Words

"Almighty and Eternal God, behold I come to the Sacrament of your only-begotten Son, our Lord Jesus Christ. As one sick I come to the physician of life; unclean to the fountain of mercy; blind to the light of eternal splendor; poor and needy to the Lord of heaven and earth."

Reader's Guide for Saint Thomas Aquinas, page 162.

Saint Elizabeth Seton

"God Is with Us"

Born: August 28, 1774, New York City

Died: January 4, 1871, Emmitsburg, Maryland

Feast Day: January 4

Patron: those who have difficulties with in-laws, children near death, loss of a parent, widows, Catholic schools, those persecuted for the Catholic faith

The raw November wind whistled through the cracks in the damp stone walls of the quarantine building as the gracious woman sat in a corner and wrote in her journal, watching over her husband and daughter. Elizabeth smiled at eight-year-old Anna as she tried to jump rope, using the piece of cord that had tied her belongings together. Anna skipped over to her father, who lay coughing on his bed. Elizabeth's smile faded. She was finding it harder to hide her anxiety for her husband, whose cough had grown so much worse in the past few days.

Elizabeth and her handsome husband had come to Italy hoping that the warm Italian sun would heal—or at least slow—his tuberculosis. Instead, officials in Livorno had quarantined them in a dank, unheated building because they feared Will might be carrying yellow fever. The unhealthy conditions had hastened her husband's decline. His good friends, the Filicchis, had provided a bed and sent food, but this help wasn't enough.

The sick man coughed again and called, "Betty!" Instantly Elizabeth was at his bedside. "Let's say our service," Will murmured. "I'll feel less chilled afterward."

As she took up her worn prayer book and called Anna to kneel with her beside the bed, the young wife marveled anew at the religious transformation that had taken place in her husband. Will had hardly ever gone to church until just a few months ago. His lack of interest in religion had been the only real cloud in their joyous and devoted relationship. Elizabeth's faith had sustained her through their recent difficulties, and she had grieved that Will didn't seem to share the strength and peace of faith. But now Will Seton had truly turned to his Savior, and Elizabeth's intense sorrow at his illness was mixed with a deep joy—even while suffering the privations of quarantine.

Devoutly, the little Episcopalian family held their daily prayer service while the wind continued to howl through the fissures in the old stone walls.

November merged with December as the dying husband and father waited for clearance. As she wrote in her diary, Elizabeth took comfort in Will's newfound faith and rejoiced that she could "wait on God" in nursing and cheering her husband.

The officials shortened the quarantine, but by the time Will was released, it was too late. He died in Pisa only two weeks later.

Philip and Anthony Filicchi and their wives welcomed Elizabeth and little Anna into their own home, as first Anna and then Elizabeth fell ill after Will's death. The Filicchis grew to admire Elizabeth greatly. They were impressed by her devotion to God, her silent grief, her care for her little daughter, and her yearning for her younger children across the ocean. The Filicchis openly lived their own—Catholic—faith and invited Elizabeth into their family prayers, hoping to comfort her.

Politely curious at first, Elizabeth gradually found herself intrigued by Catholicism. She was amazed to discover the Catholic belief in the Real Presence of Jesus in the Eucharist. When she saw how ardently her newfound friends believed, she too fell to her knees before the Blessed Sacrament carried in procession in the streets. Her yearning for a deeper, sacramental communion with God, and her gradual recognition that the Catholic Church linked directly back to the apostles, set off a storm of inner conflict. She felt drawn to enter the Catholic Church, but she knew what tremendous resistance she would face from family and friends when she returned home.

Home for Elizabeth Bayley Seton was New York. She had been born into a prominent New York family two years before the American Revolution. Her early childhood had been overshadowed by the War of Independence and her mother's untimely death, followed by her younger sister's passing. Elizabeth grew up close to her father, a busy physician who took time to guide her education. He remarried when Elizabeth was four, but Elizabeth's stepmother rejected Elizabeth and her older sister. Finally, when Elizabeth was in her teens, her father and stepmother separated. Meanwhile, Elizabeth struggled with a deep depression. Later, she would thank God for saving her from doing anything desperate. Even at a young age, Elizabeth had a deep faith that she nurtured by reading Sacred Scripture and praying the psalms.

At age nineteen, Elizabeth met and fell in love with William Seton, a young man from another prosperous, distinguished family. The fashionable young couple enjoyed several years of married bliss and social prominence, hosting a party for George Washington and being neighbors to such famous persons as Alexander Hamilton. God blessed them with five children.

But then a series of challenges faced the young family. The death of Will's father left the support of his large family (including Will's younger siblings) to Will and Elizabeth. The family's importing business declined to the point of bankruptcy. Then their children became ill, one after another. After that Elizabeth was devastated by the death of her own father.

Now, after ten unforgettable years, Elizabeth had lost Will. An impoverished widow at age twenty-nine, Elizabeth had five children under the age of nine to raise and support. Her desire to convert to Catholicism would deeply disturb her family and friends. Elizabeth could think of only one person whom she could rely on—her sister-in-law and "soul-sister," Rebecca Seton, in whose care Elizabeth had left her other children during her trip.

Accompanied by Anthony Filicchi, Elizabeth and Anna returned to New York in the early spring of 1804. Elizabeth's sorrowful heart was eased by her joyful reunion with her children—Bill, Dick, Kitty, and baby Bec. But another sorrow immediately marred her joy. Her sister-in-law was gravely ill. Only a few weeks after Elizabeth's return, Rebecca, her confidante, died of tuberculosis.

Grief, insecurity, fears for the future, and doubts became a storm raging inside Elizabeth—a struggle that she shared with her Episcopalian pastor and spiritual director, Reverend John Henry Hobart (who later became a bishop), and the Catholics she met through Anthony Filicchi. She corresponded with both Bishop Cheverus of Boston and Archbishop Carroll of Baltimore. After months of internal debate and prayer, Elizabeth made an act of faith and entered the Catholic Church on March 14, 1805. A few days later, she received Holy Communion, and wrote in her journal, "At last God is mine and I am his!"

Now one of the loneliest periods in the young widow's life began. Family and friends could not understand her conversion. Fearing that she would try to convert them, most of them shut her out of their lives. The Filicchis remained good friends, providing financial help as well as counsel, which the struggling family desperately needed. Anti-Catholic prejudice made Elizabeth's efforts to attain financial independence very difficult—whether she tried running a boarding house or teaching.

Finally, Archbishop Carroll of Maryland invited Elizabeth to come to Baltimore to open a Catholic school for girls. Elizabeth accepted his invitation. With her children at her side, she began the school under extremely poor conditions. The poverty and obscurity of those first years would have discouraged anyone—that is, anyone but Elizabeth. Somehow Elizabeth's faith gave her the courage she needed. In addition, she was highly educated, refined and well-mannered, a practical and balanced woman who was able to accomplish much.

One of her deepest joys was that, unlike in New York, it was now easy to shape her life around prayer and daily Mass, since there was a chapel right next door. Ever since she had been in Italy, Elizabeth had longed to dedicate her life to prayer and service. Her daughters were inspired by their mother's ideals and joined in her efforts even as children. Two of Elizabeth's younger sisters-in-law, Harriet and Cecilia, not only converted to

Catholicism but also came to join Elizabeth. Other young women were similarly inspired and joined her to work at the school. Without realizing it, only three and a half years after her conversion, Elizabeth was launching what would become a vast undertaking of the Catholic Church in America: the parochial school system.

In 1809 the community received a generous donation to found a school for poor children. They moved to a farm in nearby Emmitsburg, where the group continued to live with great physical hardships, yet in a Christ-centered joy under Elizabeth's inspiring leadership.

Under the guidance of Archbishop Carroll, Elizabeth and the other women gradually formed themselves into a religious community, with exceptions being made for Elizabeth to continue her responsibilities as a mother. They first took the name "Sisters of Saint Joseph," but a few years later changed the name of the growing congregation to "Sisters of Charity," basing their spirituality on the writings of Saint Vincent de Paul, which Elizabeth translated from the French. Their very name—Sisters of Charity—underscored their way of life. The long black dress, elbow-length cape and characteristic black bonnet soon became a familiar sight in schools, hospitals, and orphanages. The sisters went anywhere spiritual or corporal works of mercy were needed.

Against Elizabeth's will, and despite the fact that she had to balance the additional responsibilities of motherhood, the community always kept her as their superior. "Mother Seton" as she came to be called, wisely guided the community through the hardships of its early days and throughout its early expansion.

Elizabeth was also a prolific writer, using the distinctively feminine writing forms of her day: letters, journals, and memoirs.

Her writings are full of spiritual gems, and they trace an incredible journey of trust in God's will and love for her at each and every moment, no matter how painful the circumstances.

Elizabeth's writings also reveal one of her greatest strengths and inner beauties: her ability to build deep and abiding friendships. Yet this, too, was one of her greatest sources of suffering, for again and again she lost her dearest, closest companions—members of both her "families." Within a year of joining her, her young sisters-in-law died. This special sorrow was followed by the death of Elizabeth's own daughter Anna, who was a novice at the time. Later, her youngest daughter, Bec, would also die at Emmitsburg. Of the nearly one hundred women who joined the original congregation, Elizabeth would bury eighteen.

Elizabeth's great consolation in these sorrows was her friendship with Jesus in the Eucharist. She wrote, "What can shut us out from the love of him who will ever dwell within us through love?"

During the last three years of her life, Mother Seton grew increasingly ill and felt God inviting her to live the paschal mystery more deeply, sharing in Jesus' sufferings and death so as to share in his glorious life. On January 4, 1821, at the age of forty-six, she gave her final recommendation to her community, "Be children of the Church. Be children of the Church." And Mother Seton's soul slipped away to enjoy the perfect union with God that she had so joyfully anticipated every day in Holy Communion.

Personal Challenge

In the spirit of Saint Elizabeth, who at her first Holy Communion said, "At last God is mine and I am his," will I allow

Jesus to fill me with the same joy by placing Mass and Communion at the center of my life?

Prayer

Saint Elizabeth, many of the great joys of your life—your family life, your conversion, the fulfillment of your deep desire to dedicate your life to Christ as a religious sister—were interwoven with great sorrow: deaths of loved ones, rejection by family and friends, physical hardships, and the challenges of founding a new way of life. For you, these sorrows could be borne, accepted, and turned into treasures by your love for Jesus in the Eucharist and his love for you. Help us to accept the challenges in our own lives, trusting in God's loving presence. Amen.

Notes on Her Life

- Elizabeth's life was filled with lonely periods of loss. Her stepmother rejected her and her older sister. Later, when her father and stepmother separated, Elizabeth's depression could have led her to contemplate suicide.
- As a couple, Elizabeth and William belonged to the fashionable Trinity Episcopal Church, where Elizabeth also received spiritual direction from the pastor, the Rev. John Henry Hobart. With her sister-in-law Rebecca Seton, Elizabeth organized other women to alleviate poverty.
- Elizabeth's first question to the Filicchis about the Catholic faith stemmed from her curiosity about the words of a prayer, the "Memorare." After her conversion Elizabeth became greatly devoted to the Blessed Mother.

~::~ Tuberculosis ravaged the Seton family. Besides her husband, two of her daughters, Anna and Bec, died in Elizabeth's arms. In addition to her "soul-sister," Rebecca, two other sisters-in-law, Harriet and Cecilia, also died of tuberculosis. Elizabeth's fourth child, Catherine, was the only daughter present at her mother's death.

~::~ Elizabeth and sixteen other women pronounced their vows as Sisters of Charity for the first time in 1813.

~::~ A year later, Elizabeth sent three sisters to Philadelphia to found the first orphanage in the United States.

~::~ Elizabeth Ann Seton's writings are filled with spiritual gems that unfortunately are still not widely read.

In Her Own Words

"The greater my unworthiness, the more abundant is his mercy."

Reader's Guide for Saint Elizabeth Seton, page 164.

RECONCILIATION

Saint Rita

Saint of the Impossible

Born: ca. 1381, Roccaparena (near Cascia) in Umbria, in what is now Italy

Died: May 22, 1457, Cascia, Italian peninsula

Feast Day: May 22

Patron: impossible or desperate causes, difficult marriages, infertility, parenthood, victims of abuse

Rita finished baking the bread and setting the table for supper, then looked out the door to see if her husband, Paolo, was approaching. Not yet, so she didn't need to call her sons in from outside. Rita took a deep breath and looked up to the mountains. Despite the peaceful evening, her heart was not entirely at peace.

The endless feuding that rent the fabric of medieval Italian society had recently flared up in Cascia and its neighboring villages. Paolo's family had been involved in one such feud for generations, but though Paolo himself had a fiery temperament, he'd never directly engaged in the conflict. Cherishing this rare free moment, Rita knelt in front of the crucifix in their home. "Keep him safe, Lord. Don't let our family suffer from this feud. Bless us with peace. Bless Paolo with peace."

Rita suddenly realized it was growing dark. In her prayer, she had lost track of time, and now real anxiety gripped her. Paolo should have been home by now! She banked the fire, wrapped her shawl around her, and started to walk to meet her husband. On this beautiful evening she was too worried to stay home waiting.

On the path, Rita heard angry voices ahead. Stomach churning, she ran toward them. A neighbor appeared and tried to hold her back. "Rita, wait! You don't want to see him like this—we were just coming to tell you . . . ." But Rita shook him off and ran past him toward the awful scene awaiting her.

Paolo's body lay still on the ground, his chest covered in blood from stab wounds. One look at his face and Rita knew he was already gone. She fell to her knees, grasped his face in her hands, and kissed him. "Paolo! My Paolo!"

Tears streaming down her face, she looked up to the small circle of men. "Did you find him like this? Was he alive? Was there a priest here? Or did he die . . . alone?"

When the men could not meet her gaze, she knew the answer. Paolo had died alone. Suppose he had been afraid? Suppose he had fought? Suppose he had died with anger in his heart? Rita's fear for her husband's salvation pressed on her, choking her. Her husband, with whom she had struggled to build a life, a family, a safe circle in this mad world of violence, was gone in an instant. Grief and fear robbed her of breath and clear vision. All she could see was Paolo's frozen, empty face.

More footsteps were coming up the path. Feeling a thousand miles distant, clutching her husband's cold hand, Rita recognized first the voices, then the faces, of her husband's family. Screams of grief, roars of "Who did this?" echoed around her but didn't move her. Then, one sentence jarred her back to herself.

"When we find out who did this, they'll pay for it in blood," promised an angry voice.

"No!" Rita's horror pushed her to her feet. "Stop talking like that! How many more wives must become widows? How many more children, orphans?" She gasped for breath. "Help me bring him home. I must get back to my sons before they hear this from someone else," she pleaded.

The men carried Paolo's body behind her in a respectful, silent procession as she made her way home. Rita pulled her mind away from her own grief and horror. How could she break this news to her boys without igniting the understandable desire for revenge? Her impetuous teenage sons would be easily influenced by their relatives.

They were waiting inside for supper, eating some bread at the table when she walked in. "My sons," she said, "Father was attacked on the way home and hurt very badly. He's in the hands of God now." Rita held out her arms, and Gian Giacomo and Paolo Maria rushed into them. She held them close, heart pierced anew by the sorrow and confusion that had filled their eyes.

Somehow, Rita made it through the next couple of days. She tried to be attentive to Gian Giacomo and Paolo Maria, not leaving them alone with her husband's family, yet respecting their need for space to grieve. Rita focused her own grief by praying insistently for Paolo's entrance into heaven. But her sons grew increasingly withdrawn and seemed very tense when together.

Rita pulled them aside individually and talked to them. She invited them to come to church with her and pray for their father and his murderers—that was the word her sons insisted on using. With her mother's instinct, she could tell that her sons were being drawn into the negative cycle of revenge and violence—they seemed obsessed by it.

Rita visited her husband's family and begged them to forgive Paolo's murderers, or at least to stop speaking to her sons about revenge. When they indignantly dismissed her as weak and disloyal to Paolo's memory, the accusations wounded her deeply.

Over supper, Rita raised the subject with Gian Giacomo and Paolo Maria. "Do you think I am disloyal to your father's memory if I don't want to take revenge on his killers?"

Gian Giacomo looked away and didn't answer. Paolo Maria responded, "That's okay, Mamma. We know it's not disloyalty. We'll be strong for you."

Rita leaned forward and laid her hand on her son's. "Do you think it's easy to ask God to forgive those who killed your father and left him to die alone on the road? Forgiveness takes more strength than revenge does. I'm not being weak. I'm respecting your father's love for justice and Jesus' call to be peacemakers. Revenge is not the answer, boys. If you try to take revenge for your father's death, you will be unjust to someone else. The violence will never stop unless we take a stand and are strong enough to forgive."

At her words Paolo Maria snatched his hand away. "No! It's not fair! We lost our father! They should suffer for it!"

Rita turned to Gian Giacomo. "Don't do this! Only God can make things right! Violence isn't the answer—it just brings more violence, more death!"

Gian Giacomo shoved his half-empty plate away. "All we want is justice for our father." He stood up. "C'mon, Paolo, don't let her talk you down."

Paolo stood up with his brother, and they left the house, slamming the door behind them.

Dry-eyed, Rita cleared the table. She had no tears left. She had just lost her husband and still feared for his eternal salvation. Now it seemed her sons were lost to her—and perhaps to God as well. Waiting up for them, Rita offered the most difficult prayer a mother can.

"Lord, you know all things. And you love my sons more than I ever could. They are all I have left in this world. You know the goodness in their hearts. Don't let them go down this path of destruction and violence that will destroy them. *Anything* would be better than for them to lose their very selves in this pit of hate-filled revenge. They won't listen to me anymore, so I entrust them completely to you. Protect them from themselves, guide them to eternal happiness in you."

Shortly after Paolo Maria and Gian Giacomo had revealed their true intentions to Rita, they both fell ill. Fearing that this might be God's answer to her prayer, Rita nursed them with great dedication. *They are both young and strong; they will recover!* she thought hopefully. But their illness grew grave. Both young men came back to their senses. They confessed their murderous intentions and received the sacraments of Reconciliation and Viaticum. But tragically, neither survived. Rita lost both her sons within days of each other, less than a year after their father's death. Rita's only consolation in her great grief and loneliness was that she was sure they would enter the heavenly Father's embrace.

"What now, Lord?" she prayed. After some months, Rita found an earlier desire resurfacing. As an only daughter, Rita had followed her parents' wishes to marry so they could have her near them in their old age, while she enjoyed the protection of a strong husband and family in that feud-riddled area. However, Rita's parents had died soon after her marriage. She found it ironic that her obedience to their desires had left her so vulnerable and alone. Could she now follow her initial desire to enter the convent?

She visited the Augustinian convent in nearby Cascia and requested an interview with the abbess. The abbess listened to the request of the devout woman who was also the victim of such terrible tragedies, but kindly explained that, although widows sometimes became nuns, it was very rare at this particular convent. She told Rita to come back for an answer after she had consulted the community. When Rita returned, the abbess said she had been refused.

Greatly disappointed, Rita went home. Although there were two other convents in the area, Rita still felt that God was directing her to enter the Augustinians. She went back a second and then a third time. The last time, the abbess told her rather harshly not to return. Rita wondered whether the nuns were fearful that her family connections might bring the feud to the convent.

Rita prayed for patience, perseverance, and clarity about what to do. After some months passed, she received a vision of three saints: Nicholas of Tolentino, Augustine, and John the Baptist, who showed her the way past the closed doors of the convent. Relying on prayer and determination, Rita arranged a reconciliation between the two feuding families. After she succeeded in bringing peace, she was finally accepted into the convent. The sisters quickly discovered that Rita's spiritual maturity was evident in her wholehearted spirit of obedience and deep prayer.

In the convent, Rita's devotion to the crucified Jesus deepened, especially after she listened to a famous Franciscan, Giacomo della Marca, preach about Jesus' sufferings and death. She begged God for the grace to share everything with Jesus, even his sufferings. She felt that only in this way could she *really* become one with her divine Bridegroom. Jesus granted her desire in a singular way. While she was gazing at the crucifix, Rita felt one of the thorns from Jesus' crown pierce her forehead. The thorn created a painful, gaping wound that refused to heal. It soon festered and became repulsive, making it difficult for the other sisters to even approach Rita. Even if they could overcome their repulsion, the sisters still feared contagion. From this mystical wound, Rita suffered terrible pain and the burden of living as a virtual hermit within the community for the last fifteen years of her life. Yet, she rejoiced to share in Jesus' sufferings so directly, and she was happy to spend her life completely dedicated to prayer.

On May 22, 1457, when Rita was about seventy-six years old, she went to meet her beloved Bridegroom. The moment she died, stories of miracles started to surround this humble woman. The convent bell began to ring without anyone touching it. The room where she was laid out glowed with a heavenly light; her wound was healed and her face became fresh and youthful. Within weeks of her death, a dozen miracles took place, all attributed to her. And although Rita's body was never embalmed, it still lies incorrupt in the chapel of the convent in Cascia.

Rita is now called the saint of the impossible, because in her own life she faced so many impossible situations and in each of them found that with God all things are possible.

Personal Challenge

In the spirit of Saint Rita, choose one situation or relationship in your life where you can become a person of peace and work to bring about reconciliation.

Prayer

Saint Rita, faithful disciple of Christ, in every circumstance of your life, no matter how painful, you trusted in God. Teach me to trust in God's love, to be persistent and courageous in seeking peace and ending violence, able to see past injury and injustice to the suffering face of Christ. For only in making peace with one another can we live in union with the God whose love embraces us all. Amen.

Notes on Her Life

~::~ Rita's first biography was written over 150 years after her death, making it difficult to determine what is fact and what is legend. Additional, critical research done close to her canonization shed some surprising light on her life. What remains clear is that the many miracles attributed through Saint Rita's prayers to God confirm not only her closeness to God but also her great desire to help people who face very difficult situations.

~::~ Cascia is so small that few would have heard of it were it not for Saint Rita.

~::~ Legends tell us that Rita's parents were elderly when she was born and were known as peacemakers in the region.

- Stories that Rita's husband, Paolo, was a violent, abusive spouse were based on a mistaken reading of some writing on Rita's original coffin that was obscured by smoke stains. When the coffin was restored 500 years later, the words once thought to refer to him were found instead to refer to the great pain she suffered from her mystical wound. If Rita's parents were peacemakers concerned for her future, it is unlikely that they would have arranged for her marriage to a violent, feuding husband. Nonetheless, like every marriage, Rita's required a daily commitment of love and self-sacrifice.

- Rita's sons may have been twins.

- Another lovely legend says that when she entered the convent, the superior told Rita to water a dead stick planted in the ground. Rita did so faithfully, and the "stick" became a vine that continues to flourish today.

- A legend recounts that the nuns were persuaded to accept Rita into their community because Saints Nicholas Tolentino, Augustine, and John the Baptist escorted Rita through the convent's locked and bolted doors one night. The next morning the community found her praying in the convent chapel, with all the doors still locked and bolted. Another legend says the saints inspired her to reconcile the feuding families.

- Rita is considered a stigmatist because she truly shared physically, as well as spiritually, in Jesus' suffering.

In Her Own Words

We have no recorded words of Saint Rita. But we know of her commitment to peace and reconciliation, and her immense devotion to Jesus in his passion. Most likely the crucifix was the "book" she meditated on most frequently.

Reader's Guide for Saint Rita, page 167.

Saint Augustine

Seeker of Truth

Born: November 13, 354, Tagaste, Numidia (now Souk-Ahras, Algeria)
Died: August 28, 430, Hippo (now Annaba, Algeria)
Feast Day: August 28
Declared Doctor of the Church: 1298, by Pope Boniface VIII
Patron: brewers, printers, theologians

Alipius studied his friend's abstracted face while they ate. Augustine was his former teacher, a cherished friend, and a brother on the journey of seeking the truth. Augustine's great mind and heart had led Alipius to follow in his footsteps. And now, it was clear that Augustine's attention was wandering far from the fascinating table conversation.

Their guest for lunch, a Christian named Pontitianus, had been describing the life of a holy man, Anthony of Egypt, who was inspiring other Christians—including two of his friends—to dedicate their whole lives to God. Augustine had listened eagerly, until this point.

As Pontitianus rose to leave, Alipius said goodbye, then followed Augustine into the next room. As he entered, Augustine whipped around to his friend and almost shouted in agitation, "What are we doing, Alipius? The unlearned are seizing heaven by force, and what are we doing? We, with all our knowledge, are heartless cowards, wallowing and sinking in the mire!"

Alipius was astonished, not so much by Augustine's words but by the anguish in his eyes and tone. Augustine turned and went into the garden, and Alipius followed. He could not desert his friend, whom he had never seen so distressed.

For a while, they sat together in silence. Finally, Augustine got up and walked a short distance away. Alipius watched as his friend sank to the ground. Alipius glanced back at the house where Augustine's mother, Monica, was clearing up after their meal. Should he call her? He had never seen Augustine so upset.

Sitting alone under the fig tree, Augustine poured out years of grief and regret through his tears. Even now, when so much had finally become clear, Augustine's doubts tormented him.

His doubts had begun as a youth, when he had left his devoutly Christian mother to study at the university of Carthage. In the fourth century, it was the custom to be taught the faith, but not to receive Baptism until adulthood. The skepticism prevalent at the university made a deep impression on Augustine, and he gradually rejected the teachings of the Church as too simple and impractical to live. At age nineteen, impressed by the writings of the Roman orator Cicero, Augustine had begun his lifelong search for truth. Discounting the Christianity in which he had been raised but which he had never truly explored, he'd found himself drawn to Manichaeism, a religious cult that attempted to synthesize all known religions into one.

Brilliant as a student, Augustine had quickly become a teacher, but he continued to explore various philosophies and religions. Eventually, he became disillusioned with Manichaeism but continued to search. In his need to seek the truth without restraint, he had even deceived his mother and left for Rome without her. Eventually, he ended up teaching in Milan. Here, his mother caught up with him. Augustine had begun listening to the preaching of Ambrose, bishop of Milan, because he admired his rhetoric. But soon he found himself agreeing with much of what Ambrose was saying. Augustine started to study Christianity.

Now Augustine's intellectual doubts were finally melting away in the light of Christ. He felt he had at last found the truth. But he still wasn't ready to embrace Christianity because he felt he couldn't live the Church's teaching on purity. Augustine had been faithful to one woman for decades—a woman he had deeply loved but never married, who had given birth to his son, Adeodatus. At Monica's prodding, Augustine had recently broken up with the woman, but he found he couldn't bear the solitude, and had started living with another woman while his mother arranged for his marriage. He felt that it was too late, too hard, for him to learn to live chastely.

At lunch, Pontitianus' story about Anthony of Egypt had shone a brilliant light that cast Augustine in a deep shadow. Augustine felt he finally saw his true self—a self that was deformed by sin. How could he, with all his studies and intellect, not have the courage to embrace the truth? If others could follow Christ so single-heartedly as to leave everything behind, why couldn't he leave behind his life of sin? In the midst of his tears and self-loathing, Augustine started to pray, "How long, O Lord, how long?"

Suddenly, Augustine heard a child's voice chanting, "Take up and read! Take up and read!" Augustine looked around for the child. Seeing no one, he realized that he was hearing the voice of inspiration. Hadn't Pontitianus said that Anthony of the Desert's conversion had come from reading one line of the Gospels? Rising to his feet and going back to Alipius, Augustine picked up the Letters of Saint Paul that he'd been reading. Eagerly, like a man crazed with thirst, he opened the Scriptures and read, "Let us live honorably as in the day, not in reveling and drunkenness, not in debauchery and licentiousness, not in quarreling and jealousy. Instead, put on the Lord Jesus Christ, and make no provision for the flesh, to gratify its desires" (Rom 13:13–14). As he read the words, a light suddenly filled his entire being, dispelling not only his doubts but also his inner turmoil. Closing the book, Augustine joyfully turned to Alipius. "I'm abandoning the past and embracing Christianity!"

Alipius picked up the Letters of Saint Paul as Augustine had, and found a line that inspired him. Together, Augustine and Alipius went to tell Monica the good news. Monica hugged her son, weeping and sobbing, "Thanks be to God! At last! Thanks be to God!"

An uncontainable happiness finally filled Augustine's heart. He had been so afraid to lose the pleasures of his former life, but now they seemed like trifles compared to the delights of the spirit he enjoyed in God's love. He withdrew from public life to prepare himself for Baptism—praying, fasting, and doing penance. He wrote a prayer that revealed his regret at having waited so long before surrendering to God:

> O Jesus Christ, amiable Lord, why did I, in all my life, ever love and desire other things instead of You? Jesus, my God,

> where was I when I was not thinking of you? Oh, at least from this moment on, may my heart have no other desires than for you. O desires of my soul, hasten and run from now on, you have lingered too long already; hasten to reach the goal to which you aspired. Really seek him whom you seek. God of my heart, Divine Jesus, let my heart consume itself for you. May the glowing ember of your love burst into flame in my breast and be the beginning of a divine conflagration: may it continuously burn upon the altar of my heart, inflame the intimacy of my being and consume my entire soul, so that on the day of my death I may appear before you, consumed by love for you. Amen.

Finally, on Easter in the year 387, Bishop Ambrose of Milan baptized Augustine; he died to his former life and began his new life in Christ. Joining him were his good friend Alipius and Augustine's son, Adeodatus, who was about fifteen years old. Grateful for the treasure of new life he had received, Augustine still feared his own weakness and constantly begged God in prayer for the strength he needed to resist temptation.

Shortly after Augustine's conversion, his mother, Monica, died. Augustine returned to Tagaste, his hometown, and dedicated his life to God through a monastic life of prayer, chastity, and study. He gathered friends around him who shared in his simple lifestyle. Despite Augustine's hesitancy and protests, the bishop of Hippo ordained him a priest, and encouraged him to preach. A few years later, the bishop ordained him a bishop and proclaimed Augustine his successor.

Although he was initially hesitant and remained committed to a simple lifestyle, Augustine became an energetic and prolific herald of the Gospel, tirelessly and enthusiastically explaining, defending, and clarifying the teachings of the Church and the

Scriptures. Daily, sometimes twice a day, he preached to the faithful. More than 400 of his sermons are still in existence.

Many of Augustine's writings and sermons focused on the errors and crises of his day. He convincingly addressed the theological or philosophical errors that were popular or seemed particularly deceptive, such as Manichaeism, Donatism, Pelagianism, and Arianism. As the Roman Empire collapsed around him, Augustine wrote *City of God* to address the relationship between the kingdom of God and earthly kingdoms.

The most widely read of all his books is his *Confessions,* which Augustine wrote to share his experience of the mercy and goodness of God. He wanted others to know him as he truly was—and, in his humble opinion, to stop giving him too much credit for his new lifestyle and example. In his own words:

> The caresses of this world are more dangerous than persecutions. See what I am from this book: believe me and not what others say of me. Pray for me that God may complete what he has begun in me and that I may never destroy myself through pride and vainglory. I have written this book to incite myself and others to praise God who is ever just and good and to raise our minds and hearts to him.

Ironically, in writing his *Confessions* Augustine was not only one of the first people to write a true autobiography, but he actually created a new genre of literature: the spiritual autobiography.

At the age of seventy-six, after forty years of intense service to Christ and the Church, Augustine was stricken with a fever. Despite his fears of temptation and his own weakness, Augustine had faithfully lived his dramatic baptismal commitment to Christ. Afire with the love of God as he lay dying, he could hardly bear the vehemence of his love. What a desire he had to go to heaven, to see face-to-face the gracious God who had sought him out and won him, showering him with mercy and forgiveness; that God who had sought him relentlessly and to whom he had finally surrendered.

When he became too ill to rise from his bed, Augustine asked for the penitential psalms to be written out and hung on the wall in front of his bed. He also requested that no one visit him except the doctor and those who brought his meals. The last ten days of his life became a kind of retreat, in which he prayed the psalms continually and was moved to an even greater sorrow for his sins and more profound gratitude for God's goodness and mercy. He died peacefully on August 28, 430.

Augustine had no material goods to bequeath, for long before he had given everything away. Yet, in bridging the gap between the early Church Fathers and later Church Doctors, he left a profound legacy to the Church. His example of conversion and holiness as chronicled in his *Confessions* and his approximately forty volumes of profound theological and philosophical preaching and writings undergird the religious convictions of Christians up to the present day. Because Augustine's personal experience of God's gracious embrace shapes all of his writings, he is known as the Doctor of Grace.

Personal Challenge

In the spirit of Saint Augustine, who prayed to Jesus, "Why did I, in all my life, ever love and desire other things instead of you?" ask the Holy Spirit to show you any desires that hinder your living a full Christian life. Bring them to confession to obtain healing and strength.

Prayer

Saint Augustine, you sincerely and fearlessly sought to discover and live the Truth, no matter where your search led you. May we listen as attentively to the Word of God and respond to God's invitation as fully as you did. Help us to celebrate God's beauty, love, and goodness in our own lives to trust that God has a plan for us and that God gives us the grace to live according to it every day. May we live as you did, in continual conversion, seeking to correspond always more fully to the grace of our Baptism. Amen.

Notes on His Life

- Augustine was not an eager student in his youngest days—his parents and teachers had to force him to study.
- Augustine speaks disparagingly of the sins of his youth, but he was known to be a man of good manners and principles. He was faithful to the woman he loved—who was also the mother of his son—for many years.
- Augustine listened to Saint Ambrose because he was interested in his rhetoric. Gradually, he became intrigued with what Saint Ambrose was saying.
- Augustine's conversion journey was lengthy. He was inspired to be baptized after reading the Letter to the Romans on August 15, 386; he was baptized the following Easter, April 25, 387, at age thirty-two.
- Augustine was ordained a priest in 391, although he was very reluctant. As a priest and later as a bishop, he continued liv-

ing the monastic life; he wrote a rule of life for his priests and for the community of women he founded.

~::~ Literary milestones: his *Confessions,* published in 401; *The Trinity,* published in 420; *The City of God,* completed and published in sections from 413 to 425; his *Retractions,* a revision of his previous writings, published from 426 to 428. (Here, "published" does not mean "printed." Until the invention of the printing press in the mid-fifteenth century, books were written by hand.)

In His Own Words

"Late have I loved you, O Beauty ever ancient, ever new; late have I loved you!"

Reader's Guide for Saint Augustine, page 169.

ANOINTING OF THE SICK

Saint Alphonsa of the Immaculate Conception

The Lord's Own

BORN: August 19, 1910, Kudamaloor, a small village in Kerala, India
DIED: July 28, 1946, Bharanganam, Kerala, India
FEAST DAY: July 28
PATRON: those who are ill, death of parents

Sister Alphonsa moved restlessly on her cot. Her many ailments often made it difficult to sleep, so she had devised her own nocturnal pastime for the dragging, sleepless hours: to express her love to the One to whom she belonged. Although the sores on her legs caused her great discomfort, she focused her inner gaze on Jesus on the Cross. *For you, my Jesus,* she offered silently. *All I want is to be united to you. I am happy to suffer for you and with you.*

But something was missing from her prayer. Sister Alphonsa needed to be entirely honest with her Spouse. So she went on. *I want to ask you about my novitiate. If I don't get well, I can't continue as a novice. Father has told all the novices to pray for me, that I be healed through the intercession of the saintly priest, Father Kuriakose Elias Chavara. I would like to make novitiate so that I can belong here with you forever! But even more, I want to do your will.*

Satisfied with her prayer, Sister Alphonsa wondered what God would do. God had brought her here, to the Franciscan Clarist community, but not by the most direct path.

Sister Alphonsa was born Annakutty Muttathupandathu on August 19, 1910, in a small village in India. The youngest of four children, she'd lost her mother only weeks after her birth. Raised in turns by a loving father and grandmother, and more strictly by her aunt, her "second mother," she had received a deeply spiritual upbringing. Her family were members of the Syro-Malabar Catholic Church, a respected religious minority in India. The Syro-Malabar Church traces its origins to the missionary work of Saint Thomas the Apostle in India during the first century AD. This Church observes traditions and ceremonies of the Chaldean Rite, which developed in the ancient city of Edessa, now in Iraq.

"Annakutty," (or "little Anna"), as she was called, suffered severe eczema as a young child but eventually recovered. She made friends easily. One of her best friends at school was a Hindu girl named Lakshmikutty. (This friend would still be alive at the time of Alphonsa's canonization.)

Annakutty's aunt couldn't understand her niece. Thinking of the future, she raised her to make an advantageous marriage and become an excellent housewife. But from the age of seven, Annakutty considered herself as "given" to Jesus. She was no longer her own, but his. She often visited the Carmelite monastery near her home and felt called to religious life. But her family wouldn't hear of it. Annakutty determinedly resisted every effort her family made to persuade her not to follow her call.

Finally, her aunt began arranging a formal marriage for her. The pressure mounted so high that thirteen-year-old Annakutty came up with a desperate and misguided plan prompted by reading the lives of several saints. She would destroy some of her beauty so no one would want to marry her anymore. One night she purposefully put her foot into the hot embers of the fire pit to scar it. But she slipped and fell. Instead of receiving a superficial burn, Annakutty painfully burned both feet and legs so badly that the toes of one foot had to be surgically separated and bound. Her recovery took over a year and left her permanently disabled. Her family gradually recognized that they would not be able to change her mind about her vocation.

Annakutty's confessor guided her to the Franciscan Clarist community at Bharanganam, whose mission included teaching. On Pentecost, 1927, Annakutty arrived at the school, intending to continue her education and eventually enter the community. She entered postulancy the following year, taking the name Sister Alphonsa of the Immaculate Conception, in honor of the saint of the day, Saint Alphonsus Liguori.

For the next five years she had endured an unending succession of illnesses. She had completed her schooling, received a government license to teach elementary school, and taught for a full year. But then illness had forced her to take on smaller roles: assistant teacher, parish catechist, secretary.... Hardest of all had been waiting to enter the novitiate, but at last she had become a novice! Yet soon after that she had become so ill that her death seemed close. Alphonsa wondered if perhaps Jesus was calling her to heaven.

The blanketing darkness of the pain pressed down on Alphonsa. She began to think about Jesus' agony that dark night in the garden; this kept her from feeling so alone. She thought she might doze for a few minutes when, suddenly, a bright light shone in the room.

The brilliant figure of a man dressed in a Carmelite habit appeared—the saintly Kuriakose Elias Chavara, to whom the other novices were making a novena for her healing! Father Chavara blessed her, touched her, and spoke. "You are cured of this illness, but you will bear other sufferings." When he left, Alphonsa could feel that she was healed. The next morning, the novices and entire community rejoiced in her miraculous recovery. Alphonsa told no one about the apparition.

Sister Alphonsa was able to complete her novitiate. The day of her profession—August 12, 1936—was one of the happiest days of her life. She vowed to always live chastely, poorly, and obediently. Then she joyfully returned to her teaching duties at Bharanganam. But only weeks later, Sister Alphonsa fell ill, this time with a severe fever. The doctors suspected tuberculosis, and she suffered with it for six months. Once again, the community made novenas to Father Chavara and Saint Thérèse of Lisieux. And once again, Sister Alphonsa was miraculously cured. When her superiors pressed her for details, she reluctantly described the apparitions of both Saint Thérèse and Saint Chavara, who had healed her.

During the next nine years, Sister Alphonsa suffered a series of serious illnesses, including double pneumonia and typhoid fever. She also suffered a severe nervous shock one night when a thief invaded her room while she was ill. She was so traumatized that she lost her memory and certain basic abilities, such as reading and writing, for more than a year. Even in this fragile state, she offered her sufferings for others. Her health continued to deteriorate until September 29, 1941, when it was feared she was dying. She received the Anointing of the Sick in preparation for her death, but with the grace of the sacrament and the prayers and care of her community, she recovered her memory and started to recover her health.

Because of her kindness and cheerfulness, Sister Alphonsa was a favorite of the school children even though she only had the strength to teach them occasionally. Her room was near one of the schoolrooms, and she enjoyed watching and visiting with the children, often giving them treats of fruit.

Sister Alphonsa's frequent illnesses were misunderstood, but she bore the misunderstandings as silently as the physical pain. She often spoke of the Gospel image of the grain of wheat that falls to the earth to die and give life, or of grain being ground to become the bread of the Eucharist. She also compared herself to a leaf that falls to the ground and becomes a part of the soil to nurture other plants. Her "work" was to suffer with joy.

Despite her many illnesses, she was always smiling and patient. No one suspected how much she was suffering, and she preferred it that way—she did not want to receive special treatment. Those who visited to comfort or encourage her when she was ill found themselves comforted by her joy. Alphonsa was convinced that suffering was her path to union with Christ. She treasured every step on that path because he not only pointed it out to her, but had first walked it himself. She sincerely believed that the crosses she received were signs of Jesus' love for her—writing in her journal that a day without suffering was a day wasted. Her motto was, "I want to suffer for my Lord, who suffered for me." When her sufferings were severe, Alphonsa's deep devotion to Jesus in the Eucharist and in his Passion and Death on the Cross sustained her. She would also turn to Mary, "the woman under the cross" for strength and comfort.

In 1945, Sister Alphonsa started to suffer seriously from what would be her last illness. Tumors had spread throughout the organs of her body, and she suffered from violent convulsions and vomiting—sometimes as many as forty times a day. On July 28, 1946, fully aware that she was dying, she passed away with several sisters at her bedside. She was only thirty-five years old and could finally rejoice forever at being truly the Lord's own.

Her funeral was very small—only the sisters and a few friends and family members gathered to remember and pray for her. But her spiritual director predicted that her tomb would become a place of pilgrimage as people discovered what a holy mystic had lived in their midst. The day after her funeral, some of the school children started to pray for her intercession. When they received what they were praying for, devotion to Sister Alphonsa began to spread. So many miracles were attributed to Alphonsa's intercession after her death that she was compared to Saint Thérèse of Lisieux and became known, not as the Little Flower, but as the Passion Flower of Bharanganam.

Personal Challenge

When I am discouraged by the suffering in my life, can I trust as Saint Alphonsa did that God is at work even in this? Can I accept the joy that surrender brings?

Prayer

Saint Alphonsa, your one desire was to live God's will for your life. Suffering and illness did not take away your joy. Instead, they became your way to live a joyful self-offering to the One who gave all for you. When my sufferings discourage me, help me to recognize them as invitations to receive God's love and to offer my love to God. Help me to grow in love for Jesus crucified, who loved me and gave himself for me. Amen.

Notes on Her Life

~::~ Raised by her aunt because her mother died only a few weeks after Alphonsa's birth, Saint Alphonsa did not have a typical childhood. Although loving, her aunt was very severe and demanding.

~::~ Saint Alphonsa was a hidden saint whose holiness lay not so much in what she did as how she did it, much like Saint Thérèse of Lisieux, to whom Alphonsa had a special devotion. She was remembered by her sisters in religion as a friendly, kind sister who never complained or criticized others.

~::~ Saint Alphonsa's tomb has become a place of pilgrimage for people of all faiths.

~::~ In 1985, Sister Alphonsa was beatified along with Kuriakose Elias Chavara, to whom she had prayed for healing. Sister Alphonsa was canonized in 2008 by Pope Benedict XVI; Father Kuriakose, in 2014 by Pope Francis.

~::~ The miracle attributed to Alphonsa's intercession that was recognized for her canonization was the healing of an infant's clubfoot. Many other healings of clubfoot have been attributed to her intercession as well.

~::~ Saint Alphonsa's best friend from childhood, Lakshmikutty, was ninety-nine at the time of the saint's canonization.

~::~ Saint Alphonsa is the first woman of Indian origin to be canonized, as well as the first canonized saint of the Syro-Malabar Catholic Church.

In Her Own Words

"My beloved Lord dwells within my heart. Nobody can take him away from there!"

Reader's Guide for Saint Alphonsa, page 172.

Saint Damien de Veuster

Hell Transformed

BORN: January 3, 1840, Tremeloo, Belgium
DIED: April 15, 1889, Kalawao, Moloka'i, Hawaii
FEAST DAY: May 10
PATRON: victims of leprosy (Hansen's disease)

Hawaii, the land of palm trees, coconuts, and vibrant colored flowers, was a tropical paradise long before it became the fiftieth state. In the past, anyone going to Honolulu on the island of Oahu would find beauty, relaxation, and a friendly atmosphere, while anyone going to Moloka'i would find despair!

In the nineteenth century the northern outcrop of the island of Moloka'i, in the center of the Hawaiian chain, was a desolate region. On its rugged surface thousands of men, women, and children lived in total isolation from the rest of the world. People forced to leave their homes and families were brought to the village of Kalawao to waste away and die. Society treated them as outcasts, for they had contracted what was then considered the most terrible disease known—leprosy.

The plight of those forgotten people moved the heart of Bishop Maigret. On May 4, 1873, the bishop spoke with several missionary priests at Wailuku, on the island of Maui.

"Fathers, I had decided to grant the requests of the lepers of Moloka'i to have their own resident priest. But . . . I cannot lay this burden on any of you; it would be like sentencing a man to death."

Several priests generously volunteered for what was intended to be a temporary assignment on a rotating basis. However, at this point, a rugged young missionary jumped to his feet.

"I . . . I want to go to live there, Your Excellency!"

"Damien, do you realize what kind of assignment you're volunteering for?"

"Yes, Bishop, I do. I still want to go; I'm ready to embrace the lot of the lepers."

"Thank you, my son! You've lifted a great weight from my heart. When can you be ready?"

"I'm ready now, Your Excellency."

"Good! You can leave on the next boat in six days."

The following week, when the boat docked, Father Damien told himself, "I am here for life. I am on Moloka'i forever. I will die here—on this island."

Because of board of health regulations, anyone who contracted leprosy (now called Hansen's disease) was banished to the leper colony and had to remain there for life. However, to the thirty-three-year-old priest with only nine years of missionary experience behind him, the future gleamed brightly. Full of energy, strength, and enthusiasm, Father Damien was willing to sacrifice all the years that remained to him, for he was driven by a force greater than a human being's: the energy of divine love.

When he walked into the village of Kalawao, the young priest saw a pitiful spectacle. The people who greeted him looked less like humans and more like walking corpses, devoured by worms. Bloated and covered with sores, their bodies gave off the odor of decaying flesh.

A large wooden door creaked open at his touch. When Father Damien stepped into the one-room leprosarium, he reacted with utter shock.

"This is the hospital?" he exclaimed.

They had no doctors, no beds. Dozens of lepers lay on the floor, stretched out on mats. Flies swarmed everywhere, and the sick simply reposed in filth, with little food or water.

As the young missionary looked over the room, he said to himself: "These unfortunate ones are now my spiritual children . . . and I, in turn, am to be their father."

Immediately, Father Damien began to care for the material and especially the spiritual needs of the lepers. He found it very difficult to carry out his duties however, for every fiber of his being rebelled against the horrendous conditions.

In performing his priestly ministry—baptizing, hearing confessions, distributing Holy Communion, and anointing the sick—Father Damien often had to hold his nose, or even to run outside frequently to catch a breath of fresh air. The stench of leprous sweat nauseated him, and the fluid that leaked from the lepers' open sores caused his legs to itch so badly that he had to wear high boots to prevent such close contact. His clothes, too, began to carry the odor of leprosy, so he tried to counteract the stench by constantly smoking a pipe.

"Lord, give me strength, courage, charity . . . ." Damien prayed. "Let me help my people more, love them more, and forget myself."

Even though his senses rebelled at the encounter with each sick person, Father Damien persisted in his work among the lepers. He strove to always be cheerful although his heart was filled with sorrow over their sufferings. Every step brought him toward new miseries, but the zealous missionary wanted only to spend himself in serving God and his beloved lepers. His heart ached for their sufferings, and he turned to constant prayer for the strength he needed in his work.

And God answered his prayers. The Lord opened Damien's eyes, hands, and heart to see all the needs of his brothers and sisters. He abandoned himself ever more completely in order to serve them as much as he could.

Father Damien saw that besides the wounds of the body, his lepers experienced a more tremendous suffering—that of the soul. The people were not only discouraged by the torments of the disease, but many had also lost all hope. They felt they had nothing to live for.

The missionary knew what was lacking in the lives of some of these lepers: faith, hope, and love. Crushed by the rejection they had experienced from other people, many thought that even God hated them. As a result, they easily fell into such sins as idolatry, impurity, and brutality.

By his witness in following Christ, Father Damien's example slowly uplifted the moral climate of the entire settlement. The lepers called him Makna, which means "Father," for he was always pouring himself out as a gift to the people. He built small wooden houses for them; taught them how to raise crops; gave them food, clothing, and medicine; dressed their wounds; arranged recreational activities and religious celebrations; and even helped them organize an orchestra.

Some of the lepers began to join Father Damien in his many acts of kindness. As best they could, men would help in his building projects. Women took food to the people in greater need than themselves, offering them comfort and care. Even the children "came back to life" and began to play together.

Father Damien often taught catechism to the children, for he wanted to attend to their spiritual needs most of all. One day when he returned home from an errand, Father Damien found one of the leper girls sitting outside his door.

"Are you waiting for me, Tatila?" he asked.

"Yes, Makna Kamiano," she answered. "Please bring me Holy Communion. Please bring it to me right now."

Without any further question, the priest brought the child a consecrated host, which she devoutly received. No sooner had she finished thanking Jesus who had come into her heart than she went to meet him in heaven. Father Damien made her small coffin and dug her grave as he was doing for all the lepers who died.

As months turned into years, the Apostle of Moloka'i completely gave himself in caring for the lepers, to the point of risking his own health. Even when dressing open sores, Father Damien looked as though he were arranging a bouquet of flowers, completely forgetting himself and his own sensibilities. Once a leper in the last stages of the disease looked up to see the priest changing the soiled bandages around his waist.

"Oh, Makna," he exclaimed. "Please be cautious. My wounds are leaking, and the fluid will get on your hands."

"That's all right, Joseph," the priest replied. "I don't mind. It's more important that you have clean bandages."

"But you can get leprosy. I'm very contagious now."

"Don't be disturbed. Even if the disease seizes my body, God will give me a better one on Resurrection Day. Isn't our eternal salvation what's most important? God wills our holiness; that's what we must work for on this earth."

Father Damien wanted to be a blessing to each of the sick, body and soul, by his touch, his gentle words, and the respect he showed each person. One of the hands-on-care ministries that he lovingly provided for everyone, whether believer or not, was the Anointing of the Sick.

On a beautiful evening in his twelfth year on Moloka'i, Damien was preparing some warm water to soothe his tired feet. The work still made many demands on him in every way, but he was content. It had been a long day of visits to his sick. That afternoon he had finished the last of many houses he had been building. And he had even had time for a game with the orphan boys. Now the missionary was ready for a few minutes of well-deserved rest. He rolled up his pant cuffs and pulled off his dusty boots. Carefully he removed his socks and lifted one foot into the bucket and then the other. He looked down distractedly and noticed steam rising from the water. He dipped his fingers in the water and exclaimed, "Hotter than I thought!" Quickly he pulled up both feet and swung them over to a towel. Blisters began to appear on his red feet, but he hadn't felt a thing.

"Blessed be the good God!" he prayed. "I am now most certainly a leper. This is why my feet have been aching for so long. The disease has been incubating. Thank you, Lord." When he had volunteered to come to the leper colony, it was with awareness that he'd likely contract leprosy sooner or later. It would be a way to consummate the sacrifice he had so willingly made, to share more fully in Christ's Passion. As he prayed, Damien thought of what he still wanted to accomplish at the leprosarium before the Lord called him to heaven.

The disease progressed rapidly. Large blisters appeared on his once handsome face, and his neck became red and bloated. Initially his powerful hands were spared, so he continued directing his many projects. For three more years, Father Damien worked vigorously for the bodily and spiritual well-being of his beloved lepers.

Far from quenching his zeal, the leprosy seemed to make it blaze ever more vibrantly. He still faced many trials, and the fatigue and suffering grew more intense with each new day, yet he bore all for the love of Christ, who had died on the Cross for him and for all people.

Damien did live to see a cherished dream fulfilled. On November 14, 1888, Mother Marianne Cope of the Franciscan Sisters of Syracuse arrived at the settlement with two companions, ready to take care of the children. Another priest also came to Moloka'i, as did two generous lay volunteers, Joseph Dutton and James Sinnott. "I can die happy now," Damien said. "You will carry on the work and do it much better than I."

On April 13, 1889, a few days before Easter, Father Damien gave his soul back to God. His work was finished. He had transformed the squalor of Moloka'i into a haven of God's love. Father Damien died not only as a victim of leprosy. He died as a holocaust because of his love for Christ and for the souls of God's least ones, the lepers of Moloka'i.

Personal Challenge

Like Saint Damien, can I be an angel of mercy to those around me, especially those who are ill or homebound?

Prayer

Saint Damien, apostle and martyr of charity, teach us to value this virtue above all others, and above all our interests and plans. You learned love from the hearts of Jesus and Mary and made it the instrument of your life's work. Teach this lesson to all priests and ministers of the Church, that before and above all, love is to be poured out as an ointment on the needs of those they serve. May your example inspire all of us to spend our lives to the last breath in loving God and sharing his love with everyone. Amen.

Notes on His Life

- Father Damien was born Jozef (Jef) de Veuster to a prosperous farming family in Belgium. During his life he became proficient in Latin and Greek as well as fluent in Hawaiian, Portuguese, Spanish, French, and English.
- In 1858 he joined the Society of the Sacred Hearts of Jesus and Mary (SSCC), or Picpus Fathers (after the street in Paris where they first lived).
- In 1863 he was missioned to the Sandwich Islands (Hawaii) in place of his brother, Father Pamphile, who had been on the list for the mission but had become ill. In 1864 Father Damien was ordained a priest in Our Lady of Peace Cathedral in Honolulu. He served for nine years on the islands of

Hawaii and Oahu, and then, in 1873, volunteered for the leper colony at Kalawao, Moloka'i. Kalawao was cut off from the rest of the island of Moloka'i by sheer cliffs 2,000 to 3,600 feet high.

~::~ Father Damien cared for the sick and built for them: houses, a hospital, two orphanages, schools, meeting halls, chapels, roads, and a water conduit.

~::~ In 1884 he was diagnosed as a leper; he died five years later.

~::~ The miracles approved for his cause were both instant cures of fatal illnesses suffered by Sister Simplicia Hue, a French nun, in 1895, and Audrey Toguchi, a Hawaiian lay woman, in 1997.

~::~ In Hawaii Saint Damien's feast day is celebrated on April 15, his day of death.

~::~ He is recognized as a martyr of charity.

In His Own Words

"In tears I sow the good seed. From morning until night my heart is broken by the moral and physical misery here. But I try to always look happy in order to encourage my poor lepers."

Reader's Guide for Saint Damien, page 174.

HOLY ORDERS

Saint Noël Chabanel

God's Holy Failure

Born: February 2, 1613, Saugues, France
Died: December 8, 1649, Canada (New France)
Feast Day: October 19 in the United States, September 26 in Canada
Patron: Canada, along with the other seven North American martyrs

In the small wooden chapel of the mission of Sainte Marie, deep in the night of June 19, 1647, a lonely figure knelt at the altar rail. Jesuit missionary and priest Noël Chabanel had come to the chapel to relieve his mental torture, but the choking blackness only made his depressing thoughts clamor louder.

"I don't belong here! I've been trying for almost four years! How can I possibly be called here, to this mission?" Self-loathing at his own failure forced Noël to his aching feet, and despite his fatigue, he paced restlessly back and forth.

"I'm thirty-five years old, and I've got nothing to show for it. If I were back in France, I could be of real use. Am I just ignoring the waste of my talents? How can it be God's will that I fail so miserably at everything, that I can't even serve as a real priest to the Huron people?"

The anguish in his soul became intense. "My God! My God! Why have you abandoned me?" Exhausted by the struggle, Noël collapsed to his knees, his face bowed to the floor. He wept. How had his life come to this?

Noël Chabanel had dreamed of being sent to New France to evangelize the native peoples who had never heard of Christ. But once he'd arrived, this keenly intelligent and articulate professor of oratory had been reduced to silence, unable to learn even the basics of the Huron language. The Gospel that he so urgently wanted to preach was reduced to a garbled stutter. And he wasn't able to adjust to the close communal lifestyle of the indigenous people, either. The smells and noise constantly distressed him; his queasy stomach couldn't digest the unfamiliar food; the lack of privacy was torturous to his reticent nature. To pray, he had to get up before dawn or go deep into the woods. An avid intellectual, Noël couldn't even read or study in the smoky, dim, and crowded Huron dwellings.

Many of the Huron people despised him for his apparent ignorance and inability to adapt to their language and customs. They mocked him, calling him the "palest of the pale faces." When he compared himself to the other missionaries, Noël felt ashamed. In his own eyes—and, he wondered, in the eyes of his fellow Jesuits, too?—he was completely useless.

His fellow missionaries suffered the same hardships and raw life in the wilderness and faced the same travel hazards and dangers of death from the Hurons' enemies, the Iroquois. Yet, the other Jesuits were able to preach and minister tirelessly. These heroic companions even desired martyrdom if that would bring more native people to genuinely encounter Christ. Noël, instead, didn't yearn for martyrdom. He feared he would not be worthy of it. He would fail at being a martyr, as he was failing at everything else.

A cold sweat bathed Noël's body as he battled the tidal wave of depression engulfing him. "I haven't instructed one convert nor heard a single confession. What is my priesthood for? I'm lost in this wilderness. I suppose . . . I could ask to return to France. I'd be able to do some good there. But then . . . what if I would be running away from God's will? Despite everything, my superiors haven't sent me back."

The cruelest torture of all was that the one thing that had always sustained him until now had failed him: his prayer had become the source of his deepest anguish. For almost as long as he'd been in New France, Noël had been drowning in a sea of spiritual darkness. The God to whom he had given his life seemed remote, unreachable.

Tonight, Noël's shattered heart and spirit could take no more. How long he crouched there, he would never know. Finally, one prayer came spontaneously to his lips. Noël looked toward the tabernacle and cried aloud, "My God, what do you want of me?"

A gleam of moonlight revealed the faint outline of the tabernacle. The closeness of the tabernacle, of Jesus in the Eucharist, pierced Noël's soul. He suddenly knew that it didn't matter to God what he could or couldn't do. God simply wanted him, his heart, his life. Grace poured into his broken-open heart. He raised himself up on his knees and reached for the large crucifix in his robe, pressing it to his lips. "Lord, I'm nailed to the cross with you. Help me. With your grace, I will not come down."

But was this spontaneous prayer enough? Noël searched his heart. How could he strengthen his resolution to never give up, to share in the Passion and Death of his Lord as long as he was allowed, no matter how much discouragement or suffering he would face? Suddenly, he knew what he could do.

"Jesus Christ, my Savior, you have willed me to be a helper of the apostles in this Huron vineyard. I am most unworthy of this call. But I trust in you and in the designs of your holy will in serving the Huron people. I, Noël Chabanel, vow to remain here in the Huron Mission until the end of my life if my superiors so dispose. Accept me, O Lord, as a permanent servant of this mission. Make me worthy of so great a ministry. Amen."

It was the morning of June 20, 1647, and the feast of Corpus Christi. The light of dawn chased the night from the village, the chapel, and Noël's heart. He would stay. It didn't matter that he would continue to feel useless and inadequate, physically revolted, and humiliated. His vow didn't remove the natural aversion that he would feel until his death, but it made him stronger. Every new day would bring fresh ways that he could offer himself to Jesus Crucified for the sake of the Huron people. He would accept ministering in the shadows of the other missionaries. He would refuse to give up. He would give himself completely to God's will, no matter what he felt.

For the next two years, Father Noël Chabanel faithfully lived his vow. He celebrated Mass. He baptized only the sick and the dying. He continued to suffer from the harsh conditions, the demanding physical labor, and the painful lack of privacy. The absence of pure drinking water left him constantly thirsty. The steady diet of boiled corn paste, acorns and roots, indigestible to his weak stomach, left him continually weak. The feelings of inadequacy and his spiritual darkness continued to haunt him daily, but his determination remained unchanged. His ministry, his martyrdom, would be a hidden one.

In the fall of 1648, Father Noël was sent to assist Father Jean de Brébeuf at the Mission of Saint Ignatius. Fully aware of the growing menace from the hostile Iroquois warriors, Noël confided to his spiritual director, "I don't know what is happening to me or what God wants of me, but I feel that death is not far off. Yet I'm not afraid. This state of mind has not come from me, for I've always been afraid."

As he was saying goodbye, his last words to his spiritual director were, "Father Chastellain, I hope to really give myself entirely to God this time, once and for all!"

Later that day, Father Pierre Chastellain remarked to a passing priest at the mission, "I'm deeply moved after speaking with that good priest. Father Chabanel's voice and appearance just now were indeed those of one making an offering of himself. I don't know what lies in God's providence for him, but I do know this: God wants that man to be a great saint."

In February 1649, Father Noël was replaced by Father Gabriel Lalemant and sent to assist Father Charles Garnier in evangelizing a related tribe, the Tionontati, at a more remote and dangerous mission. Shortly after Noël left, the Mission of Saint Ignatius was attacked, and Fathers de Brébeuf and Lalemant were martyred. Noël wrote in a letter to his brother Pierre, also a Jesuit priest back in France:

"As you have already read in our reports, [The Jesuit Relations], Father Gabriel Lalemant merited the honor of martyrdom. Only a month before, I was in the same settlement. (You were robbed of the privilege of being the brother of a martyr.)

Father Lalemant had been assigned to relieve me since I was physically stronger, and I was sent to a more difficult mission. I was not worthy of the crown he won. My turn will come, if it pleases God, and if I try to live my own 'bloodless martyrdom in the darkness.'"

Nine months later, the Jesuit superior, Father Ragueneau, not wanting to risk the lives of both priests at the Tionontati mission, sent word for Father Noël to return to the main mission. But Noël was hesitant about leaving. He didn't want to abandon Father Garnier or the Tionontati people at a time of suffering and danger. Nevertheless, Father Garnier insisted that Noël obey their superior. On Sunday, December 5, 1649, Father Noël celebrated Mass and reluctantly embraced Father Garnier in farewell.

"I am going to where obedience calls me . . . . I must serve God faithfully until death." Then he set off with a few Huron warriors, and late in the afternoon reached the mission of Saint Matthias, twelve miles away. He would not know that the warring Iroquois would swoop down the following day and slaughter the people of the Tionontati mission, including Father Garnier. The following day Father Noël continued on his journey with a party of Hurons, traveling more than eighteen miles over dangerous and difficult trails. Nightfall forced them to take refuge in a heavily wooded area near the river. The Hurons fell asleep right away, but Father Chabanel kept watch in prayer. Despite his spiritual desolation, he was at peace. He clung to his hope and desire that finally he would be able to offer himself totally to God.

At about midnight, Noël heard noises in the distance—the victorious whoops of Iroquois and the cries of their captives. He woke his Huron companions, and they fled, circling around the Iroquois and heading back to Saint Matthias. But Noël was unable to keep up. Not wanting to slow their escape, he told them to go on without him.

The Hurons left him behind and eventually reached Saint Matthias to report what had happened. In the meantime, Father Noël hid in a clump of trees and passed the night alone. At sunrise, he set out again for the main mission but was unable to cross the river, which was too deep. A Huron, Louis Honareenhax, appeared and offered to take the priest across in his canoe. Father Noël welcomed the offer and had followed him just a few steps when the Huron suddenly turned and attacked him with his tomahawk, killing him outright. He threw Father Noël's body into the Nottawasaga River and took his belongings. It was the morning of December 8, 1649.

Father Noël's body was never found. It took two years for Noël's superior, Father Ragueneau, to confirm his suspicions of how his priest had died. The truth became known only when witnesses heard Honareenhax brag that he had rid the world of the despised priest out of hatred for the Christian faith.

In many ways, Saint Noël Chabanel's martyrdom was unique. He had lived without the spiritual consolations or feelings of accomplishment shared by his fellow Jesuit missionaries. He hadn't had anything to sustain his self-offering other than faith and surrender to grace—a grace that he rarely felt. Daily, Father Noel had struggled with feelings of aversion, sadness, disgust, discouragement, inadequacy—perhaps even despair. According to the world's standards, Noël Chabanel was a failure, a "zero." Even his martyrdom was unwitnessed except by his assassin, and his body was never found.

But Noël's deepest desire, purified in the crucible of desolation, was to fulfill his priestly and missionary calling and give himself completely to God in service of the Huron people. By God's standards and by Noël's, his life was a complete success. This "zero" belonged to God. And that was all that mattered.

Personal Challenge

Like Saint Noël Chabanel, can I trust in God's plans for me and the work he gives me, even when I see nothing, even when there are no positive results?

Prayer

Saint Noël Chabanel, you faithfully fulfilled your priestly vocation in the difficult and dangerous life of a missionary, despite the interior darkness you continuously suffered. Help all priests who face difficulties and temptations to be as open to God's grace as you were. When I am discouraged, help me remember and cling to God's faithful love, so that I may faithfully live my calling to serve and give myself to God always more fully. Amen.

Notes on His Life

~::~ Saint Noël Chabanel is one of the eight North American martyrs but is usually mentioned last. In contrast to the length and visible success of the missionary activities of Jesuits Brebeuf, Daniel, Garnier, and Jogues, the tangible achievements of the other Jesuit missionaries—Lalemant, Goupil, de la Lande, and Chabanel—are much less. However, all of them are known for their perseverance and suffering.

~::~ Noël entered the Jesuits at age seventeen and was ordained at age twenty-six. His older brother Pierre was also a Jesuit.

~::~ His superiors in France described Noël as: "Serious by nature; energetic; great stability; better than average intelligence." Because they hadn't wanted to lose him, he had had to ask twice before he was sent as a missionary to New France.

~::~ Noël arrived in New France when he was thirty.

~::~ Unable to learn the Hurons' language or adapt to their way of life, Noël lived the missionary life for six years. Meanwhile, he was enduring the dark night of the soul.

In His Own Words

> "May it be for good and all this time, that I give myself to God; and may I belong to him."

—Words spoken by Saint Noël Chabanel to his spiritual director shortly before his death

Reader's Guide for Saint Noël Chabanel, page 177.

Saint Thomas Becket

All or Nothing

Born: December 21, 1118, Cheapside, London, England

Died: December 29, 1170, as martyr in Canterbury Cathedral, Canterbury, England

Feast Day: December 29

Patron: diocesan priests; Exeter College, Oxford

It was a lovely dawn, heralding a glorious day. Both of their horses, well-rested and eager to join the hunt, were snorting and prancing about. "Now, beauty! Remember you are a royal mount," King Henry II of England exhorted as he patted the horse's neck. Poised and turning to his chancellor, Thomas Becket, the king suddenly nudged his horse, and it bolted forward. Soon both riders were jostling for position as their horses galloped toward the woods.

Henry was a brilliant, capable ruler and recognized the same intelligence and ability in his friend and chancellor. Thomas was twelve years older than his king, but people declared that the pair had one heart and one mind. At lighter moments they were as playful as schoolboys. But the good of the kingdom was uppermost in the minds of both men.

When they reached the designated spot and were taking a break before the hunt, the young king searched the face of his companion. *Yes,* he thought, *Thomas is in an exceptionally good mood today. I'll just tell him clearly that he must be the new archbishop* and *do my bidding. But not right now; I'll wait till we're returning home.*

Archbishop Theobald of Canterbury had just passed away. Henry had nominated Thomas to be his replacement, planning to use his friend to obtain full control of the revenues of the diocese and monasteries and to make the royal court supreme in Church matters. But would the people accept Thomas? Despite Thomas' lavish display of pomp and ceremony as the chancellor of England, the man's character was impeccable. Although worldly, he was not licentious like so many others. No one could impugn his integrity. Improper conduct and foul speech angered him, and he often severely punished these failings in others. This versatile and capable administrator would make a fine archbishop. He would do anything for his king. Henry was sure of Thomas . . . or was he?

"Thomas," the king said as they returned from the hunt, "I want you to be the new archbishop of Canterbury."

Thomas twisted halfway around in his saddle and stared at Henry.

"What! What type of man do you think I am to be placed in that holy office? And besides that, I know your plans for the Church. You will assert claims which I would surely oppose if I were archbishop. If such a thing happened through God's designs,

I am very sure that you would speedily change your tune. The great love now existing between us would turn to black hatred!"

Abruptly, Thomas spurred his horse on and rode the rest of the way home in sullen silence.

Well, thought Henry, *he's always opposed my schemes against the Church anyway. But he'll think twice before he opposes me as archbishop. I'll make him pay dearly.*

Thomas was eventually forced to accept the appointment and was ordained bishop in 1162. Yes, he had been a dazzling, successful young man and always showed a smiling front to the world. But the king, who thought he knew him, hadn't known the real Thomas. Henry hadn't witnessed the day that Thomas revealed to a friend that his courtly grandeur made him weary of existence and stirred in him a longing for death and heaven. His friend had been puzzled. How could such a worldly man, surrounded as Thomas was with the coarser vices of court life, escape all these untouched?

One day he received an answer to his unspoken question.

A nobleman who came to London to have an appointment with the chancellor, told Thomas' friend this story:

"I set out for London well before sunrise. At dawn I reached the cathedral and saw a figure lying prostrate at the entrance. This startled me. Just then I got a fit of sneezing, and the figure quickly stirred and rose. I couldn't see his face but noticed his stature. He was tall and slim and wore costly robes. The mysterious man intrigued me, and I was determined to find out who he was. All day I kept a close watch on the people I met. In the afternoon, I went to see the chancellor. As Sir Thomas arose to greet me, I knew right away that he was my mystery man. He must really be an extraordinary person."

Thomas' friend smiled and, shaking his head, responded, "He is indeed!"

When Thomas became the archbishop of Canterbury, a great outward change took place. The first thing he did was to resign his chancellorship. He removed from his appearance and lifestyle all signs of lavish display and pomp. He intensified the severe penances he had been performing in secret. Under his simple cassock, coarse woolen undergarments irritated and bruised his body as they had done when hidden under his rich apparel as chancellor. He fasted and prayed constantly to be strong in the struggle with the king that he foresaw as inevitable. Every evening, he invited in and personally served the poor who came to his door begging for alms. Anyone and everyone could approach the kindly archbishop, and they were sure of receiving some material or spiritual consolation.

Estrangement from the king came just as Thomas had predicted, for the archbishop constantly opposed Henry's attempts to control Church matters. Henry retaliated by persecuting his once-beloved friend and forcing him to pay fines and taxes. The king intended to settle once and for all his rule over the Church in England, so he called a meeting. That day, after much discussion and cajoling, Henry convinced Thomas that he, the king, only meant to uphold the correct order between the Church and the kingdom. Believing the king to be sincere, Thomas acquiesced.

The next day, when the written details of the king's demands were circulated as the Constitutions of Clarendon, Thomas read through them and was stunned. It seemed that in this one act King Henry had absorbed all the rights of the Church! He, Thomas, as the papal legate, could not lead the other bishops into this trap. He proclaimed to everyone with him, "By God Almighty, my seal shall never be put to such papers!"

Having no other recourse, Thomas fled across the English Channel to seek refuge in France. Once there he went to Sens to ask permission from Pope Alexander III (who was in France at the time) to accept his resignation as archbishop. By this point, Thomas was a pathetic sight—tired and discouraged, as he begged to be relieved of his heavy responsibility. The Holy Father looked at Thomas in his moment of weakness and knew what kind of a man he really was.

"No," the Pope responded gently. "You must stay at your post and defend the rights of the Church."

Thomas seemed to gain new strength as he gazed into the understanding eyes of his spiritual father. He would obey at any cost. But for now the struggle for power would continue in his absence, with the Pope attempting to bring about peace. Thomas temporarily took up residence in a Cistercian monastery.

Meanwhile, back in England, Henry was fuming with rage. He confiscated all of Becket's property and banished his relatives into exile. He even threatened the monks in France who were sheltering the holy archbishop. This turmoil lasted six years. Finally, a truce was made between the king and Thomas, even though neither agreed to compromise.

Thomas returned to England amid jubilant cries and enthusiasm from his flock. The truce, however, lasted about two weeks. Then the king heard that Thomas had clashed with him again. He had censured the bishops who had sided with the king against the Church. He had also nullified several appointments and decisions that had been made against his wishes and had worked against the good of the Church. The excommunicated bishops sent messengers to the king with lies and accusations against Thomas. In a fit of anger the king shouted, "Oh, the cowards who eat at my table! Isn't there anyone among them to rid me of this troublesome archbishop?"

Four knights took the king's words at face value. They, too, had grievances against the archbishop. They seized their opportunity to wreak vengeance under the cloak of loyalty to the king. Soon they had mounted and were galloping toward Canterbury.

First, the knights burst into the archbishop's residence and demanded to see him. They found him in his room praying and angrily repeated the accusations they had heard. When Thomas replied calmly and firmly, the four stormed out while the archbishop's servants quickly led their master into the presumed sanctuary of the cathedral.

Soon, accompanied by a well-armed and noisy crowd, the knights pounded on the locked cathedral doors. Calmly, the archbishop told the sacristan to open them. "The doors to God's house must not be barred," he said. The four men lunged forward and froze in their tracks. The crowd pressed in around them.

"Whom are you looking for?" asked the archbishop from the altar steps.

"For Thomas the traitor," cried out one. "For the archbishop!"

"I am here. Not a traitor, but archbishop and God's priest."

With that, the scoundrels rushed forward and tried to drag Thomas out of the church. The archbishop's servants put up a struggle, but, not being armed, they couldn't protect him for long. Thomas was buffeted by blows and pierced by sword-thrusts. "I commend myself to God and holy Mary," he cried. Falling to his knees, he prayed, "Into your hands, my God, I commend my spirit." Then came the final thrust. His last words were, "For the name of Jesus and the defense of the Church, I am ready to die."

When the king learned of the murder, he was devastated and deeply regretted what his thoughtless exclamation had caused. For forty days he fasted and was subjected to public penance. It is said that he made reparation for the rest of his life.

Nine years before, Thomas had told Henry, "I have fully served my king; now as archbishop, I shall serve my Church." The former civil servant had become a totally dedicated servant of the Church. Thomas was canonized only three years after his martyrdom.

Zeal for the law of the Lord had inspired Thomas Becket, as centuries before it had inspired the Psalmist:

Princes persecute me without cause,
but my heart stands in awe of your words.
I hope for your salvation, O LORD,
    and I fulfill your commandments (Ps 119:161, 166).

Personal Challenge

Like Saint Thomas Becket, can I be true to the person God calls me to be, even when it demands heroism?

Prayer

Saint Thomas Becket, holy archbishop of Canterbury, martyr of God's Church, help us to be steadfast in our faith. We do not want to compromise anything of what we hold to be true, but the pressure to bow to the prevailing culture is difficult to resist. Teach us integrity of heart, strength of character, and devotion to prayer. Pray for us that we too may withstand all persecution, great or small, and remain loyal to God's kingdom, despite any sacrifice that may entail. Amen.

Notes on His Life

- He is also known as Thomas à Becket, Thomas of Canterbury, or Thomas of London.
- After his studies he became a clerk, was later attached to the household of the archbishop of Canterbury, and studied canon law.
- Thomas Becket was named archdeacon of Canterbury in 1154 and appointed lord chancellor of England a year later.
- In 1162, King Henry II nominated him archbishop of Canterbury. Thomas was then ordained a priest on June 2, 1162, and consecrated a bishop the following day.
- Several times he prophesied his own martyrdom.
- He was twice exiled and found refuge in the Cistercian monastery in Pontigny, France.
- Saint Thomas Becket is venerated in both the Catholic Church and the Anglican Communion.
- The pilgrims in Geoffrey Chaucer's *Canterbury Tales* are on the way to Becket's shrine: "*the hooly blissful martir for to seke.*"
- T. S. Eliot wrote *Murder in the Cathedral,* a play about Saint Thomas Becket.
- Becket's parents are buried in Old Saint Paul's Cathedral.

In His Own Words

> "Pray for us that our faith fail not in tribulation, and that we may safely say with the Apostle that neither death nor life, nor angels nor any creature shall be able to separate us from the love of God, which has subjected us to affliction until he comes who will come, and will do with us according to his mercy, and will lead us into the land of promise, the land flowing with milk and honey."

Reader's Guide for Saint Thomas Becket, page 179.

MATRIMONY

Saint Peter To Rot

An "Extraordinarily Ordinary" Man

Born: ca. 1912, Rakunai, East New Britain (part of modern Papua New Guinea)
Died: a Friday in July 1945 in a prison camp near his village
Feast Day: July 7
Canonized: October 19, 2025

Peter To Rot sat in darkness, puzzling over the sad events of the day. Since bombing and invasion by the Japanese military forces almost a year before, his world had been turned upside down. The first time the Tolai people had ever seen a plane overhead, it had rained down destruction. The Japanese had completely conquered this part of Papua New Guinea and had set up their military command center in the nearby town of Rabaul. The Second World War, so far away at first, had now engulfed Peter's homeland.

At first, Peter had gained strength from the faith and leadership of the people's missionary priest, Father Lauffer, who had simply gone about his pastoral ministry, encouraging Peter to do the same.

But today, the Japanese had come and taken away *all* the missionaries in the region. Father Lauffer had shaken hands with Peter and told him, "To Rot, look after your people. Help them so they don't forget about God." As the soldiers led Father Lauffer away, the villagers had turned to Peter with dismayed expressions. He had done the best he could to hide his inner shakiness. He loved being a catechist, instructing others in the faith, listening to others' needs, and helping where he could, so he had put on a brave front for the sake of the village.

Now, in the darkness of night, when no one nearby needed his strength and his comforting words, Peter trembled under the crushing burden of nurturing the faith of all the Catholics in the Rakunai district.

A soft hand rested on the back of his neck in the familiar way. Without turning around, To Rot reached up and grasped his wife's hand in his own.

"What will I do?" he whispered. "Everyone is counting on me, but I feel so alone."

Paula's hand tightened around his, as she knelt beside him on the ground. Her lips touched his ear.

"You are not alone, To Rot," she whispered. "God is with you. I am with you."

The comfort of her touch and her renewed promise to stand by him eased the band of pressure around his chest. He turned to her, barely able to see her profile in the moonless night. She knew him best of all. In the early years of their marriage, they had often argued. He'd thought he knew best, and once he had even tried to force her to do what he wanted. How he regretted that! She had seen him at his worst, yet she had stayed with him. Their love had grown since that stressful time—even their weaknesses had strengthened their love for each other. Now, Paula seemed to know what he needed better than he did. She held out her arms to him. Peter leaned toward her, finding strength and comfort in her embrace.

The next day, he and Paula prayed their morning prayers together. Then Peter started gathering food. His first duty would be to find out exactly where the missionaries were being kept and what supplies they needed. Paula watched him with a half-smile. She couldn't help worrying, but she shared her husband's faith that God would be with them.

However, as the months passed the Japanese military grew more oppressive. Paula started worrying that Peter was manifesting his faith too openly. At first, he had been able to work with the occupying authorities. He had carried out his usual rounds of teaching, counseling, serving the poor and needy, baptizing infants, and leading Sunday eucharistic services, even after the school and church had been deliberately destroyed. Although the villagers couldn't have Mass without a priest, when Peter To Rot brought food to the missionaries, the priests provided him with the Eucharist. He hid the consecrated hosts in a secret underground cave, along with his Bible and some prayer books. Thus, he had been able to lead Sunday services for the villagers with readings from the Word of God, followed by Communion.

But lately the military had become more hostile toward Christians who practiced their faith. The military police had begun to imprison, beat, and execute people for what had been permitted only months before. Some of the villagers were becoming spies for the military. Peter had been harassed and brought in for questioning several times. And now, Catholics were forbidden to worship publicly. The police were also discouraging people from praying in their homes. What would Peter do?

Once again under the safe cover of darkness, Paula talked to her beloved husband.

"We cannot stop practicing our faith," Peter insisted.

"Of course not," Paula retorted. "But you can be more prudent. Please, Peter! I want our children to know their father." And to make her point, she gently rubbed her belly, just starting to show the new life she carried—their third child.

Even in the darkness, Paula could see the proud smile that lit Peter's face. He kissed her. Then his face sobered. "I will try. I think perhaps, if we meet in small groups, we can worship in the underground caves that we dug after the bombings started. And," he added casually, "I've asked Louise, a young girl from the village, to come by every day to look in on you, just in case."

Paula's heart double-thumped at his unfinished thought, "just in case of . . . *what?*" But she knew that Peter could not continue his work as a catechist without risk. She was aware that with all that he was doing, he worried about her and the children most of all. She leaned against him, cherishing this moment of safety and closeness.

Peter didn't tell Paula that he'd also asked Louise, who had no immediate connection to his family, to hide his religious books and the church records in case he was imprisoned.

The family's greatest trial came quickly. The military suspected that Catholics were still worshiping in secret. In their desire to gain the people's goodwill and simultaneously destroy their connection to the Catholic faith, they legalized polygamy and began to encourage it. Polygamy had become virtually nonexistent as a result of fifty years of evangelization in the village, but some of the local men, eager for a second wife, started abducting girls—including Catholics—and forcing them into marriage.

Peter couldn't stand by silently. The faith of his people was at risk. He continued his pastoral work in secret but publicly disagreed with the legalization of polygamy, openly arguing with his older brother. He affirmed the sanctity of marriage and marital fidelity. And he tried to prevent young Catholic women from entering polygamous marriages.

One of the villagers, To Metapa, especially resented Peter. The catechist had opposed To Metapa's efforts to compel a Catholic girl to become his second wife. One day To Metapa met a young couple from another village on the road. They were giggling as they walked, and, after a few probing questions, he learned that they had just been married, with Peter officiating. This was what To Metapa had been looking for. He reported Peter to the Japanese military.

Immediately, Peter was taken from his family, and his two brothers were also arrested. All three brothers were interrogated and beaten. Peter's older brother was accused of attending church and assigned to work in the labor camp for a month, after which he was released. Peter's younger brother was beaten unconscious, then released two weeks later, due to his physical condition. But the military police felt that Peter was the greatest threat. After beating him mercilessly, they charged him with opposing the officially sanctioned policy of polygamy and with leading religious services. They sentenced him to six weeks in prison. But when his prison term should have ended, they refused to tell Peter when he would be released, despite the inquiries of his village chief and another local official. Peter himself did not believe they would release him.

Peter's jailors informed him that a Japanese doctor would bring him some medicine the following day. Peter had only a slight cold, nothing that required medicine prescribed by a doctor. Suspecting that something was wrong, he asked for his shaving kit, his best clothes, his cross, and his rosary. The next day, Paula brought what he had asked for, along with some food and their two children: Andreas, six years old, and Rufina, three. Paula became distressed when Peter wouldn't eat much of the food she had brought. Knowing the real reason for her anxiety, he tried to calm her, telling her it was his duty to die for his people and for the name of the Father, Son, and Holy Spirit. The little family huddled together as long as they could, the pregnant Paula refusing to leave him. Finally, Peter told her it was time to take the children home.

That afternoon, Peter's elderly mother came to visit, and Peter told her about his suspicions. Earlier in his imprisonment, he had told his friends, "I am in prison because of those who were unfaithful to their marriage vows and because of those who do not want the growth of God's kingdom."

Later in the afternoon, Peter shaved and dressed in his best clothes, keeping his cross and rosary close by. That evening the guards took all of the prisoners out of the camp except Peter and another man they had overlooked, Arap To Binabak. When the guards found To Binabak still in the camp, they directed him to leave as well. Peter was then forced to lie down and injected with poison. When he went into convulsions, the guards suffocated him. Because Arap To Binabak walked away very slowly and kept looking back, he witnessed Peter's martyrdom. He joined the other prisoners, who were kept outside the camp all night, and told a few of them what he had seen. Later some ventured in and found Peter's body, as Arap To Binabak had described. Out of fear, none of them told anyone.

The next morning, the returned prisoners found Peter's body carefully rearranged. The prison authorities pretended to be surprised and said that he had died of an infection. They allowed Peter's family to take the body, which on examination showed that he had been poisoned and suffocated. Fear of military reprisal did not prevent a large crowd from gathering to honor this young husband and father, even though his burial was silent, with no religious ceremony allowed.

On January 17, 1995, when Pope Saint John Paul II beatified Peter To Rot in his home country of Papua New Guinea, his daughter Rufina was present. Rufina, who had been only three when her father had died defending his faith and the sanctity of marriage, would often repeat her aunt's testimony the best: "He was extraordinarily ordinary!" Thirty years later, Saint Peter To Rot was canonized as the first saint of Papua New Guinea.

Personal Challenge

Like Saint Peter, am I willing to go against the values of the world in order to live the uncompromising and challenging beauty that is marriage?

Prayer

Saint Peter To Rot, Christ was the center of your life and family. You were a loving father and husband, a dedicated catechist, who courageously and faithfully lived your vocation in humility amid the ordinary moments of married life. You chose to witness to the sanctity of marriage in the face of death. In these times when the sacredness of marriage and family life is frequently denied, inspire us to a deeper understanding of the sacrament of Matrimony and the blessing of family life. Assist all married couples to live their vows with the same love, respect, and devotion that you shared with your wife and with your people. Amen.

Notes on His Life

~::~ Peter was admired and loved as a catechist not only because he lived what he taught, but also because he was accessible and especially sympathetic for those who were in need or away from the faith.

~::~ Although well educated for a man of his village, Peter was a humble man living a simple life. During his lifetime, he never traveled more than thirty miles from his place of birth.

~::~ Peter was devoted to the Bible, carrying it with him and quoting it frequently.

~::~ The lack of written records about Peter's life is due to the oral nature of the culture of Papua New Guinea and the destruction of church records during the Japanese military occupation.

~::~ The only certain date we have in Peter's life is the date of his marriage to Paula Ia Varpit: November 11, 1936. The marriage—arranged by the family—was celebrated not only religiously but with many local customs, including the groom's gift of fifty strings of shells to his bride.

~::~ At first, the young couple argued a lot. Paula admitted that much of their fighting was due to how hardheaded she was. Gradually, as their love for each other grew, neighbors noticed how devoted to one another the couple had become. Paula died in 1993.

~::~ Peter was the father of three children. His firstborn son, Andreas, died at a young age, and Peter's third child, a son born after his martyrdom, died in infancy. Peter's daughter Rufina was the only living member of the immediate family to witness her father's beatification. Other family members have supported the cause for Peter's beatification and canonization.

~::~ Peter To Rot is the first canonized saint of Papua New Guinea.

In His Own Words

"I am a catechist and only doing my duty. If I die, I die for my faith."

Reader's Guide for Saint Peter To Rot, page 181.

Saint Zélie and Saint Louis Martin

A Family of Saints

Zélie Martin (born Zélie Guerin)

Born: December 23, 1831, Gandelain, France

Died: August 28, 1877, of breast cancer

Louis Martin

Born: August 22, 1823, Bordeaux, France

Died: July 29, 1894

Canonized together: October 18, 2015

Feast Day: July 12

Patrons: married couples, widowers, parents, those facing illness and death

Zélie Martin sat upright in the chair of the doctor's office on that never-to-be-forgotten day in October 1876. She waited patiently for his verdict. Without raising his eyes, the doctor cleared his throat and began writing out a prescription. He said, "Madame, what you have is a tumor."

"Please be direct with me, doctor. What is the use of the prescription?"

"Really, no use at all," admitted the doctor.

"Will an operation help me?"

"I'm afraid not, Madame. We have diagnosed you too late."

Dazed, Zélie stood up, mumbled words of thanks to the doctor, and slowly made her way home.

Home was a comfortable house in Alençon, France, where she and her husband, Louis, were raising their five daughters, and from which Zélie ran her successful lacemaking business. Zélie tried to focus on finishing an order for lace. She had gone to the doctor by herself, so only she knew the dreadful truth about her illness.

Exteriorly she remained calm and serene, but anguish tore at her heart. "What will poor Louis do without me?" she thought. "What will happen to Marie, Pauline, my poor Léonie, Céline, and baby Thérèse? How will they manage when I'm not here? I cannot leave them like this. I must remain for a little while longer. I must live!"

Suppertime arrived. Louis led the family in prayer, and everyone sat down to the delicious meal. Little Thérèse sat perched on her highchair, eager to begin eating. Zélie swallowed hard as she looked at her little one.

After supper was over and the dishes washed, Zélie found a moment to sit quietly with Louis and tell him what the doctor had said. As she choked out the words, Louis dropped his unlit pipe onto his lap. Eyes filling with tears, he rose, walked over to her, and embraced her.

"I want to tell the children," Zélie told him. "I may live for years, but it would be well to prepare them . . . ." Louis held her close until her tears stopped, and she leaned against him. Finally, Zélie looked up at him. Louis nodded, and together they walked into the living room to join their daughters. Marie, sixteen, was old enough to run the household and was already taking care of her little sisters. Fifteen-year-old Pauline was away at boarding school, but Zélie knew how much the news would affect the daughter with whom she was so close. At thirteen, Léonie had already been expelled from school three times, despite Zélie's best efforts. Céline was seven and Thérèse, three. They would be too young to understand. Gathering all her courage, Zélie told her daughters the bad news.

The scene was so pitiful. Zélie suffered more for her loved ones than for herself. Poor Louis just looked from Zélie to the circle of children and then back to her. Marie and Léonie sobbed inconsolably. Then Léonie ran to fling her arms around her mother's neck. She knew her mother would understand her unspoken words. Céline and Thérèse looked puzzled and wondered what this was all about. They had never seen everyone so sad before.

Zélie alone remained dry-eyed although her heart was breaking. After a few moments, she picked up some needlework and quietly set about it. Her outward serenity eventually managed to calm the other members of the family. Zélie would not pain her devoted husband and children by showing them the depths of her own sorrow and fear.

Their little family was no stranger to sorrow. In the past ten years, Zélie's and Louis' fathers had both died. Tragically, the Martins had lost four of their nine children. First, their two little boys had died, each within a year of his birth. Then their vivacious five-year-old daughter, Marie-Hélène, had passed away within twenty-four hours of falling ill. Finally, the wet nurse hired to feed their eighth child had neglected her; she had died of malnutrition in her mother's arms at only eight weeks old. Zélie had feared that little Thérèse would follow in her sisters' footsteps, but she had survived and grown strong. Both Zélie and Louis had been devastated by the death of their children and would reminisce about Marie-Hélène. They counted on their innocent children being in heaven and often prayed for their intercession in family needs.

Zélie knew what a blow her medical news was for Louis. They were so close, and they shared so much, on such a deep level. He had sold his business to help her run hers, and he never complained. How well they complemented each other—her passion, energy, and intelligence were matched by his strength, patience, affection, and orderly way of working. From their earliest days of acquaintance, they had agreed that their marriage was to be a mutual journey to holiness, and they had prayed for their children to consecrate their lives to God.

Zélie watched Louis anxiously during the next few days, fearful that he might collapse under his grief. But after his initial reaction, and a deep seriousness that overcame him, the only changes in Louis were his greater tenderness toward her and abandonment of his usual activities—even fishing. He refused to leave Zélie alone for any length of time.

At first, the busy round of household tasks and the prosperous lacemaking business continued as usual. Even though Zélie had not felt well for some time, her energetic creativity, combined with her desire to provide for her family, became a helpful outlet. But gradually, her greater preoccupation became providing for her children's welfare and helping to manage the burden that would fall on her beloved Louis' shoulders. Together, they decided to sell her lace business, so Louis could devote himself to nursing his wife and caring for their daughters.

They both prayed for acceptance of God's will but still hoped for a cure. Zélie went to Paris to visit her brother Isidore and to seek a second doctor's opinion. But the doctor only confirmed that it was indeed too late for surgery. After some months, as Zélie's strength failed and the pain grew greater, she and Louis decided she should visit Lourdes to pray for a miraculous healing. Zélie took her three oldest daughters on this pilgrimage of faith. It was a difficult trip—two of the girls got train-sick; Marie and Pauline lost their favorite rosaries; Zélie fell and injured her neck. Disappointingly, despite the baths and prayers, Zélie was not cured. During the journey home, Zélie tried to comfort her daughters, who were deeply distraught, by reminding them of Our Lady's promise to Bernadette, "I will not make you happy in this world, but in the next."

As Zélie stepped down from the train, she could see Louis waiting, holding hands with their two youngest daughters. She saw the hope in his face fade as she walked toward him—she knew the lines on her own face had deepened even in the short time she'd been away. She leaned into his gentle hug and resolved to live in the same spirit of faith she'd just witnessed in his eyes. *How could she let go of everything—not just her health and abilities, but her children?* Louis, swallowing tears, whispered in a shaken voice for her ears alone. "Welcome back, my dear. I won't leave your side again," he promised. And he didn't.

Louis became a rock of strength that Zélie clung to as her sufferings rapidly grew worse. She went to Mass for the last time on the first Friday of August. A few weeks later, she lay dying.

Louis left her side only to call for a priest, who anointed Zélie and gave her Viaticum. All five daughters knelt silently by her bed, crying. Zélie could no longer speak, so Louis comforted them.

At one point, Zélie fixed a long look of supplication on her young sister-in-law, Céline, who understood immediately and pressed her hand. "I will be there for your daughters," she assured Zélie.

Louis, Marie, Pauline, Léonie, and Zélie's brother Isidore stayed with her through the last agonizing night. Zélie died on August 28, at 12:30 A.M., surrounded by their love. The next morning, Louis performed the heartrending task of bringing his younger daughters to kiss their mother for the last time.

That moment almost broke him. He and Zélie had been married almost twenty years, and, though he had been a determined bachelor when he had met her, Zélie's beauty—inner and outer—had quickly attracted him. They had truly become as one. What would he do without his partner in life's adventure? How could he raise their five daughters on his own?

Louis would have preferred to remain in his beloved Alençon, where he had friends and support. But Zélie had wanted him to take the girls to Lisieux, so they could be near their Aunt Céline and Uncle Isidore. They would greatly need a motherly figure in their lives. Now widowed at fifty-four, Louis focused on raising his five daughters, ranging in age from four to seventeen. He had never felt so lost. Daily, he took sanctuary in a little attic apartment the girls called "the Belvedere," where he could read and pray.

But he didn't allow his grief to weigh on his daughters. Rather, he made sure to take tender care of them. He encouraged them to keep their little family customs, such as gathering around the fireplace in the evening to read a carefully chosen spiritual book before going to bed. He still sang to little Thérèse while she sat on his lap. Céline chose Marie as her "little mother," and Thérèse chose Pauline as hers. An affectionate and loving father, Louis' attentiveness to his daughters' needs gradually helped heal the family's grief. He'd always had a special relationship with each of his daughters, giving each a pet name. He was closest to his oldest daughter, Marie, whom he called his "diamond." Pauline was his "pearl," Léonie was "Good Léonie," Céline "his dauntless one," and Thérèse, "little Queen." Their home continued to be a tranquil "holy ground" for his daughters to nourish themselves spiritually and prepare for their vocations.

In 1881, Pauline, who had always expressed an interest in becoming a religious, discerned her vocation to the Carmelites. Louis gave her permission to enter. Four years later, both Léonie and Marie also asked their father's permission to enter religious life. To give permission was a great sacrifice—Céline and Thérèse were still young, even though Céline was ready to run the household. But above all, Louis would miss his daughters. Touchingly, he opened his heart to Marie, the daughter he'd always confided most in. While he encouraged her in her vocation, he also revealed that her going would be his greatest sacrifice because he had thought she would never leave him.

Louis' health gradually began to deteriorate, and he suffered a minor stroke. Around this time his youngest daughter, fifteen-year-old Thérèse, asked permission to enter Carmel. Not so much surprised, but grief-stricken once again at the thought of such an early separation, Louis picked a little white flower and handed it to her, explaining how God had showered it with love. From then on, Thérèse thought of herself as that little flower.

Although Céline also secretly desired to enter Carmel, she decided she would be the one to stay with her father through all the trials of his illness. After Thérèse entered Carmel, Louis began to suffer from the effects of cerebral arteriosclerosis. He started wandering off where no one could find him. Realizing that she could no longer take care of him because she couldn't watch him all the time, Céline sorrowfully brought her father to a psychiatric hospital run by the Sisters of Charity of Saint Vincent de Paul, who only allowed her to visit him once a week. Louis offered to God the humiliation of being institutionalized. Three years later, when his health had declined further and he could no longer wander off on his own, Céline brought him home to care for him.

He continued to gradually decline, visiting his daughters at Carmel one last time. On Sunday, July 29, 1894, at age seventy, Louis died a peaceful death, rejoining his beloved wife Zélie and their four children already in heaven.

Zélie and Louis Martin's deepest desires were granted. All five of their surviving daughters dedicated their lives to God in religious life. The youngest would one day be known as *Saint Thérèse of the Child Jesus,* more popularly called the *Little Flower,* and declared a doctor of the Church. Saint Thérèse would refer to her parents as "holy ground" in which she and her sisters grew up.

Personal Challenge

Like Saint Zélie and Saint Louis, whose personal holiness was a beacon to their five children, can I see my own life choices and decisions as helping my friends and family to a life of holiness?

Prayer

Saints Louis and Zélie, hear our prayers for our family. You tenderly nurtured your littlest ones into health and holiness, and you also knew how to encourage the best in your loved ones. You generously entrusted your family into the loving hands of God, not allowing the stresses of demanding commitments to business and loved ones to fracture your love for each other nor the peace of your home. In the difficulties we face as a family, help us to grow together in love, so that our family may truly become the place where we become saints. Amen.

Notes on Their Lives

~::~ Zélie described her own childhood as "sad as a winding-sheet." Her mother was very strict and wouldn't even allow her two daughters to have dolls.

~::~ Both Louis and Zélie wanted to become religious before they met each other. They didn't because. . . .

Louis was told he couldn't enter the Carthusians since he didn't know Latin; after some months of studying, he gave up.

Zélie was probably refused because of ill health; her only sister became a Visitation sister and later provided guidance for Léonie, who entered that community.

~::~ Louis had been a confirmed bachelor, but within three months of meeting Zélie, he married her. Louis was thirty-five, Zélie twenty-seven.

~::~ Despite her longing for religious life, Zélie would later say that she was born to be a mother since she loved her children so much.

~::~ Louis and Zélie had nine children, but only five girls survived. (They lost two boys and two girls under the age of six.) The cause for their third daughter, Leonie, was opened in 2015, and Leonie is now a Servant of God.

~::~ Both parents paid close attention to their children's individual qualities, seeking to help them develop. Zélie's observations can be found in her letters (more than 200 of them remain); Louis nurtured a unique rapport with each of his daughters that grew as they matured.

~::~ Zélie Martin was a working mother who oversaw the work of a number of young women weekly. Louis also ran his own successful watchmaking/jewelry business, but eventually sold it so he could support Zélie's lacemaking—as accountant, manager, and salesman.

~::~ Louis and Zélie Martin were the first married couple and parents to be canonized together.

Motto for Their Marriage Inspired by Saint Joan of Arc

"God is served first."

Reader's Guide for Saint Louis and Saint Zélie, page 183.

Reader's Guides

Saint Paul

Baptism: Newness of Life

A sincere young Pharisee finds himself on the wrong side of truth. His life after conversion is a living illustration of the power of Baptism.

Discussion Questions

- Do you know the date you received the sacrament of Baptism? Are there ways to celebrate that anniversary in a meaningful way?
- Paul brought the message of salvation to many different peoples. Each of the baptized is charged with the mission of bringing others to Jesus Christ. What are practical ways of sharing the faith with someone you know?
- Christianity is marked by joy, peace, and love, yet Saul was told that he would have to suffer for his belief (Acts 9:16). Can you give personal examples of how these two things can go together?

- ~::~ Saul was transfixed both by the look of peace on the face of Stephen as he was being stoned and the love radiating from the face of Jesus, whom he encountered on the road to Damascus. After meditating on this encounter with love, can you see how this experience of Paul could make a difference in your prayer life and in your relationships with others?
- ~::~ Do you ever think about the amazing gift of your Baptism? How could recalling this gift more frequently enrich the meaning of your life?

Read ~::~ Reflect ~::~ Respond

All his life Paul remembered the mercy he had been shown. Read 1 Timothy 1:12–17, a reflection on the renewal of Paul's life by God's inexhaustible love and grace through Jesus Christ, who transformed him from a persecutor into an apostle. Praying with this passage, we find it also speaking to the Baptism in which we ourselves have received the abundance of Christ's grace poured out upon us.

In his letter to the Corinthians Paul speaks about the unity of the members of the Church with Christ who is head of the Body, a unity brought about by Baptism that incorporates us into the Church and makes us members of the Body of Christ. Delve deeper into the Church as the Body of Christ by reading 1 Corinthians 10:16–17; *Catechism of the Catholic Church* 787–790, 1227, 1263.

Saint Cecilia

Baptism: Newness of Life

As a young woman of her time, Cecilia submitted to her parents' plans for her marriage; as a Christian, she was obedient to Christ. She catechized her husband and her brother-in-law, and together with them she gave the ultimate witness of faith.

Discussion Questions

~::~ In the story, Cecilia makes this statement when telling Valerian about the importance of her Christian faith: "I believe that Jesus Christ is the Son of God, who came down from heaven to share our human life with us. He died to save us, to save me, from sin and despair and suffering. I've been in love with him my whole life." How would you state to someone in three sentences what it means for you to be a Christian?

~::~ The Sculptor Stefano Maderno created a striking statue of how Saint Cecilia's body was found when she was exhumed a second time in 1599, and the sculpture is still on display in the Basilica of Saint Cecilia in Trastevere (Rome). Cecilia is shown lying face down with her hands in front of her. One finger on the left hand is extended and three fingers on the right; these represent the unity and Trinity of God. This is how Cecilia witnessed to her faith and renewed her baptismal promises. In what ways can you witness to your Baptism?

~::~ Before reading this story, how did you understand the meaning and power of Baptism in your life? Had you ever thought about the way that "Baptism is the basis of the whole Christian life" (CCC 1213)?

~::~ Do you think of yourself as fearlessly living your Baptism? Why or why not? How can you live your Baptism more fully?

Read ~::~ Reflect ~::~ Respond

Saint Cecilia knew the grace she had received with her Baptism. Look more deeply into the way Baptism brings about our entrance into the life of the Most Holy Trinity by reading Matthew 5:14; 28:18–19 and *Catechism of the Catholic Church* 3, 1239.

Cecilia made a vow of virginity when she was still very young. Explore how both the sacrament of Matrimony and the practice of virginity for the Kingdom of God come from the Lord himself by reading *Catechism of the Catholic Church* 1619–1620.

Saint Helena

Confirmation: An Increase and Deepening of Baptismal Grace

Helena was a woman of tremendous charity. Even in her suffering, she had a depth of goodness that was clearly the work of the Holy Spirit. Faithful to the inspirations she received, she lifted high the cross of Christ.

Discussion Questions

- Is there a specific part of this story that inspires you to pray to the Holy Spirit for strength to witness more completely to Christ in your life?
- The *Catechism of the Catholic Church* states that in Confirmation "you have received the spiritual seal, the spirit of wisdom and understanding, the spirit of right judgment and courage, the spirit of knowledge and reverence, the spirit of holy fear in God's presence" (CCC 1303). In Saint Helena's story, how did these gifts of the Holy Spirit help her navigate life's difficult and challenging situations? How can relying on these gifts help you in your own life?
- Helena became a Christian when she was sixty-three. As a witness of Christ and a sign of her belonging to the Church, she immediately began to care for the needy poor in the city of Rome. The sacrament of Confirmation gives a special strength to witness to Jesus in the world and to assume the responsibilities of Christian life. Have you ever thought that you too have your own

particular way of being Christ's disciple in the world today? What is unique about the way you witness to Christ with the strength and grace of your Confirmation?

~::~ Popular legend claims that Helena discovered the Cross of Jesus while in the Holy Land preparing ground for a new church. Whether or not this is true, she did discover the true meaning of the Cross during her pilgrimage to the Holy Land. After enduring many sufferings in her life, she found peace of heart as she walked in the footsteps of Jesus, learning to unite her sufferings to those of Jesus on the Cross. What is most challenging for you about the suffering in your own life or in the life of someone you love? What has been enlightening and encouraging to you about Saint Helena's love for the Cross of Jesus?

Read ~::~ Reflect ~::~ Respond

The effect of the sacrament of Confirmation is the special outpouring of the Holy Spirit that was once granted to the apostles on the day of Pentecost. Take a moment to remember your own Confirmation, and ponder more deeply the way this sacrament deepens baptismal grace, reflecting on Luke 24:45–53; Ephesians 1:13–14; *Catechism of the Catholic Church* 1302–1305.

The sacrament of Confirmation leads the Christian "toward a more intimate union with Christ and a more lively familiarity with the Holy Spirit" (CCC 1309). After reflecting on the Scripture passages above and the references from the *Catechism of the Catholic Church*, consider how you have grown in holiness in the years since your Confirmation. For further reflection, read Luke 4:18–19; John 17:21–23; 20:21–22; *Catechism of the Catholic Church* 1308–1309.

Saint Lorenzo Ruiz

Confirmation: An Increase and Deepening of Baptismal Grace

Everything seemed to go wrong for this young Catholic husband and father. Yet in the midst of an unbelievable situation he called on the grace of his Confirmation and received the ultimate reward.

Discussion Questions

~::~ Lorenzo had come face-to-face with death unwittingly and unwillingly. His story is a perfect witness to the power of the sacrament of Confirmation because, after struggling against his fate, he prayed for strength and found himself filled with holy purpose. In his martyrdom he won the greatest victory. Share occasions when you felt the power of your Confirmation.

~::~ Before he escaped to Japan, Lorenzo was falsely accused of murder. The occupying Spaniards picked him out because he was half Chinese and half Filipino and thus considered a second-class citizen. At Pentecost the Holy Spirit descended on people of every background. In what way have you—or people you know—experienced the power of the Holy Spirit in respecting and welcoming the "other" into your own life or into a group you belong to?

~::~ Lorenzo was an ordinary Catholic who was placed in a situation that called for extraordinary courage. It was through the power of the gifts of the Holy Spirit, which he had received in his Baptism and Confirmation, that Lorenzo was able to move beyond his fear and achieve the ultimate purpose of his life in that moment of severe trial. Though you may never find yourself in such a drastic situation, there will be times when you will need the gifts of the Holy Spirit in order to live your faith in your workplace, in your family, in civic and public life, and/or in the Church. After reading the story of Lorenzo Ruiz, how do you view the power of the Holy Spirit in your life with new eyes?

~::~ Without any knowledge of where he was going, Lorenzo boarded a ship to escape capture. One week after the ship docked in Okinawa, he and the Christian missionaries were picked up and imprisoned by the Japanese authorities. While being tortured, Lorenzo experienced great fear. Have you ever been tempted to pretend you were not Catholic out of fear or to avoid some ridicule or prejudice? What aspects of Lorenzo's personal experience can be helpful for living and witnessing as a follower of Jesus Christ in today's world?

Read ~::~ Reflect ~::~ Respond

"I am a Christian, and I shall die for God. For him, I would give a thousand lives, if I had them." These last words of Lorenzo Ruiz to his judges before his martyrdom almost surprise us with their courage and determination. They are a true sign of the presence and power of the Spirit. To understand more clearly how the seal of the Holy Spirit "marks our total belonging to Christ, our enrollment in his service for ever" (CCC 1296), read Luke

24:36–49; Acts 1:8; Ephesians 6:10–20; *Catechism of the Catholic Church* 1285, 1296.

The Sacrament of Confirmation prepares us to give bold witness to our faith in Christ and to willingly surrender our lives to him. The martyr bears supreme witness to Christ, who died and is risen, a witness given even unto death. Reflecting on Lorenzo's supreme witness of martyrdom and the following selections, think practically about how you are being called to live as a confirmed member of the Catholic Church. Read 2 Corinthians 2:14–17; 2 Maccabees 6:18–28; *Catechism of the Catholic Church* 2473–2474.

Saint Thomas Aquinas

Eucharist: Source and Summit of Christian Life

One of the Church's greatest theologians, Thomas Aquinas wrote works of theology that still sustain our faith, as well as eloquent hymns that express the Church's eucharistic belief and devotion. His intellectual astuteness was matched only by his humility of heart.

Discussion Questions

~::~ The lines of the prayer that speak about the eucharistic mystery as "a sacred banquet in which we receive Christ himself, renew our memory of his suffering and dying for us, and rejoice in the promise of future glory of everlasting union with God," are from the text for the Feast of Corpus Christi attributed to Saint Thomas Aquinas. These words express the way Thomas Aquinas understood the Eucharist, and they are also used to describe the Eucharist in the *Catechism of the Catholic Church*. How did you understand the Eucharist before reading this chapter? Does this prayer of Aquinas give you greater insight into Mass and Holy Communion? In what way?

~::~ How does reading about Thomas' experience of Jesus while praying before the Blessed Sacrament make you think about your own relationship with Jesus? How would you explain to others your belief in the Real Presence of Jesus in the Eucharist?

~::~ Thomas Aquinas, with all his learning, experience, and holiness, brought his questions and his work to the chapel to offer them to Jesus present in the Eucharist. After writing about the Eucharist, he prayed: "Lord Jesus Christ, I humbly beg of you, if what I have written of this most holy Mystery is true, say so. But if it is not, please stop me from going further." Upon hearing the way Thomas opened up his heart to Jesus in the Eucharist, and Jesus' response to him in the story, what was your initial reaction? Why?

~::~ After reading about Thomas' relationship with Jesus, what do you hope will change in your own relationship with Jesus in the Eucharist?

Read ~::~ Reflect ~::~ Respond

It is no surprise that Thomas Aquinas' humility disposed him to deep contemplative prayer. Contemplative prayer is a gift, a union with the prayer of Christ who conforms us to himself and draws us into the life of the Holy Trinity. Learn more about how to pray with your faith fixed on Jesus by reading Matthew 6:19–21; 18:1–4; *Catechism of the Catholic Church* 2711–2719.

In order to leave us a pledge of his love, Jesus instituted the Eucharist. Through this gift he remains with us always, and we are made sharers in his Paschal Mystery. In the spirit of Thomas Aquinas and to enter more deeply into the Mass and eucharistic adoration, study the biblical texts and the teaching of the Church on the Eucharist, reflecting on John 6:35, 54–56; Luke 24:13–32; 1 Corinthians 11:23–27; *Catechism of the Catholic Church* 1322, 1337, 1380–1381.

Saint Elizabeth Seton

Eucharist: Source and Summit of Christian Life

Elizabeth Seton began life as a wealthy New Yorker, enjoying her husband and children within a busy social circle. Tragedy left her widowed and poor, but God gave her the treasure of faith and called her to be a religious foundress and mother to many.

Discussion Questions

~::~ What difference would it make to your participation at Mass if you were as amazed at the Catholic belief in the Real Presence of Jesus in the Eucharist as Elizabeth Seton was? Have you ever felt a yearning for the deeper communion with God that Elizabeth wrote about in her journal after receiving Holy Communion for the first time: "At last God is mine and I am his!" What is most meaningful to you about the moments after Communion?

~::~ In sorrow over the deaths of her young sisters-in-law and daughters, as well as several women who joined her community, Elizabeth's great consolation was her friendship with Jesus in the Eucharist. Have you experienced for yourself the transformation that eucharistic devotion and belief in Jesus' love and Real Presence can make? Have you witnessed this in the lives of others? In what way?

~::~ Looking at the arc of Elizabeth Seton's life, it is impossible to overestimate how characterized it was by suffering. Many times, no simple explanation or solution could have enabled her life to go on "as usual." Sufferings were an inexplicable part of the mystery of her life, of her discovery of the Catholic faith and Jesus' love for her in the Eucharist, and of the outpouring of her life for others. She experienced always more deeply how she was sharing in Jesus' sufferings and death so as to share in his glorious life. Have you ever thought of your own sufferings as part of the larger mystery of your life? As having meaning through a sharing in Jesus' own suffering?

~::~ After Elizabeth's husband died, Philip and Anthony Filicchi and their wives welcomed Elizabeth and little Anna into their home. They openly lived their own faith and shared it with her. Eventually they stood by her in her need after her conversion, providing for her struggling family. Who has been instrumental in your journey of faith? How could you be a helpful presence and instrument of God's grace and presence for others?

Read ~::~ Reflect ~::~ Respond

"The Church knows that the Lord comes even now in his Eucharist and that he is there in our midst" (CCC 1404). The Eucharist is a pledge of future glory as it "makes us live for ever in Jesus Christ" (CCC 1405). Take some time to learn more about the eucharistic presence of Christ and deepen your devotion to the Eucharist by reflecting on Matthew 26:26–29; Revelation 19:7–9; Luke 24:13–35; *Catechism of the Catholic Church* 1374, 1376–1378, 1404–1405.

In the Gospel of John, Jesus invites us to receive him in the sacrament of the Eucharist. Expand your appreciation of the fruits of Holy Communion by reflecting on John 6:53–58; 15:5; 1 Corinthians 10:16–17; Revelation 3:20; *Catechism of the Catholic Church* 1391–1393, 1397.

Saint Rita

Reconciliation: Return to My Father

In Rita's time many animosities took root among the regions and neighborhoods of Italy. Justice was administered by local families, and feuds often proved deadly. Rita made it her mission to bring about reconciliation rather than revenge.

Discussion Questions

- After reading Rita's story, how do you understand these words of the Our Father in your own life: "Forgive us our trespasses as we forgive those who trespass against us"?
- Rita is now seen as "the saint of the impossible" because she faced so many impossible situations, and in each she found that with God all things are possible. Share times when reliance on God worked a "miracle" for you or for someone you know. How do you see these situations differently after reading the story of Saint Rita?
- In difficult circumstances of life, Rita trusted in God. She was courageous in seeking peace and ending violence. Does reading the story of Rita make it easier to see how trusting in God and taking courageous action can go together? What challenges you about her example?
- Paolo's relatives and Rita's sons accused her of weakness when she would not seek to avenge her husband's death. Rita responded that "forgiveness takes more strength than revenge." You may live through situations and relationships that are so trying or traumatic that revenge seems

the only way to right the wrong. What is illuminating to you about Saint Rita's example? How does Rita's story offer strength and comfort in difficult situations?

Read ~::~ Reflect ~::~ Respond

Growing in virtue requires God's help, practice, and perseverance. Because it is not easy for us to practice virtue, particularly in the difficult situations of our lives, we need to receive the sacraments frequently and seek to follow God's inspirations. Reflect upon your own life while exploring the virtues that Saint Rita practiced. Read Matthew 5:43–45; Ephesians 4:23–32; Galatians 5:22–6:1; *Catechism of the Catholic Church* 1810–1811, 1803–1804, 1808, 2302–2306.

The story of Saint Rita is an example of how God in Christ brings about a new creation by reconciling us to God. Each of our life stories is unique, just as Rita and the members of her family had to make their own journeys to reconciliation. Deepen your desire to be a reconciler by reflecting on these selections: 2 Corinthians 5:17–21; Romans 16:17–20; Job 12:10; *Catechism of the Catholic Church* 1489, 2838–2845.

Saint Augustine

Reconciliation: Return to My Father

Augustine went from being a self-confessed sinner to one of the most influential figures in Church history—he is known as the Doctor of Grace. His *Confessions* have been instrumental in reconciling many persons with the Church.

Discussion Questions

- As he struggled with the idea of conversion, Augustine cried out, "How long, O Lord?" The answer he received was, "Take up and read." He picked up the Bible and read, "Let us live honorably. . . . Put on the Lord Jesus Christ, and make no provision for the flesh" (Rom 13:13–14). In which way do you find it most difficult to respond to the Lord's call in your life? In Augustine's story, what gives you the most hope?

- After listening to Pontitianus, Augustine asked himself how he, with all his studies and intellect, didn't have the courage to embrace the truth. If others could follow Christ so single-heartedly as to leave everything behind, why couldn't he leave behind his life of sin? What parts of Augustine's journey were the most illuminating for you? What rings true for you?

- After Augustine's conversion, he decided to dedicate his life to God through a monastic life, but after a few years was ordained a bishop. He became an energetic and prolific herald of the Gospel, tirelessly explaining the teaching of the Church and the Scriptures. The book called his *Confessions* has helped many to be reconciled with God. Have you gained insights by viewing your own spiritual journey through the lens of Augustine's life?

~::~ Augustine wrote a prayer that revealed his regret at having waited so long before surrendering to God: "O Jesus Christ, amiable Lord, why did I, in all my life, ever love and desire other things instead of you?" Have you ever experienced this regret, particularly when preparing for the sacrament of Reconciliation? In what ways are the other things you desire promising a happiness that only God can provide?

Read ~::~ Reflect ~::~ Respond

Jesus was sent by the Father because God loved the world. He offers his mercy to all, forgiving the sins of everyone who seeks him. To receive his mercy, we need to come before him honestly, admitting our sins. Augustine knew well that the God who created us without our cooperation will not save us without it. Deepen your understanding of God's call to conversion and his love and mercy by praying the penitential psalms that Augustine had written on the walls of his sickroom before he died. They are Psalms 6, 32, 38, 51, 102, 130, 143. You might also like to pray with or reflect on Joel 2:12; Luke 15:32; 19:10; Acts 17:27; *Catechism of the Catholic Church* 1846–1851.

In his letter to the Philippians, Paul urges us to think of "whatever is true, whatever is honorable, whatever is just, whatever is pure" (Phil 4:8). Delve into the Scriptures and Church teachings for guidance in growing in virtue and holiness, by reading Psalm 119:9; Matthew 5:8; Romans 13:14; 2 Corinthians 3:17; 6:3–10; Philippians 4:8; *Catechism of the Catholic Church* 1804, 1809, 2517–2520.

Saint Alphonsa of the Immaculate Conception

Anointing of the Sick: Sacrament of Healing, Strength, and Peace

Instead of marriage, this daughter of India desired to consecrate herself entirely to Christ as a religious. Constant bouts of illness threatened to put an end to her desire until she received several visions confirming her choice. Suffering continued, but so did her witness of joyful offering, a grace she received in the Anointing of the Sick.

Discussion Questions

- "By the sacred anointing of the sick and the prayer of the priests the whole Church commends those who are ill to the suffering and glorified Lord, that he may raise them up and save them" (CCC 1499). "As soon as anyone of the faithful begins to be in danger of death from sickness or old age, the fitting time for him to receive this sacrament has certainly already arrived" (CCC 1514). This sacrament of healing unites the sick person to the Passion of Christ, brings strength and peace, forgives sins, spiritually (and sometimes even physically) heals, and prepares the person to pass over to eternal life. Before you read this story, how did you understand the importance of prayer and the sacraments for persons who are seriously ill or elderly? What is your appreciation for this presence of the Church and the sacraments now?

~::~ What are some of the clues in the story of Alphonsa that point to a person's dignity regardless of one's condition of health, mental capacity, or ability to work? Share something of your own experience. In what way is Saint Alphonsa's experience a confirmation of your own? In what way does it challenge you? How did you consider the suffering in your own life or that of others before reading the story of Alphonsa? How do you consider it now?

~::~ Does Saint Alphonsa's courageous joy draw you? Have you already experienced this joy? What is your secret for making a self-offering to Jesus during times of suffering?

Read ~::~ Reflect ~::~ Respond

The Anointing of the Sick commends the sick to the Lord so he might "raise them up and save them." It strengthens them to unite their sufferings to the passion and death of Jesus. Deepen your understanding of God's mercy as offered in this sacrament by reflecting on Isaiah 38:16–17; 57:18–19; Mark 6:13; John 11:25–26; 1 John 2:27; James 5:14–16; Revelation 21:1–7; *Catechism of the Catholic Church* 1499, 1514–1515, 1517, 1531–1532.

Experiences of suffering, injustice, and death can shake our faith. The Church's ministry can help a person turn to what is most essential. Explore the wisdom of the Church around the difficult realities of suffering and death by reading Psalms 48, 121; Isaiah 38:16–17; Philippians 4:6; Luke 8:50; 1 Corinthians 13:12; 2 Corinthians 4:13–18; 2 Timothy 2:11–12; 1 John 3:2; *Catechism of the Catholic Church* 163–165, 1500–1501, 1521, 1528–1529.

Saint Damien de Veuster

Anointing of the Sick: Preparing for the Journey Home

Strong and energetic, this young priest generously gave himself for the spiritual and material good of the leper colony on Moloka'i. Nothing seemed too much for him. He spent himself completely and joyfully until he was totally identified with his people, becoming a leper with them.

Discussion Questions

~::~ Christ's compassion toward the sick and his many healings recounted in the Gospels are a sign that the Kingdom of God is among us. Damien was the presence of Christ to the lepers who had been abandoned on Moloka'i. What indications of the presence of God's Kingdom may be found in the story as Damien begins to minister to the lepers? Have you ever considered or experienced the beauty of ministry to the sick or gravely ill in your family or parish?

~::~ In the story a young girl asks Damien to bring her Holy Communion immediately, and after thanking Jesus she dies. The Church prepares persons for death by offering them—besides Penance/Reconciliation and the Anointing of the Sick—the Eucharist as Viaticum, "the seed of eternal life and the power of resurrection." As Christ died and rose, so Viaticum is "the sacrament of passing over from death to life" (CCC 1524). Before reading this story how did you appreciate the three sacraments by which the Church prepares a person to complete their earthly pilgrimage? How do you appreciate them now?

- Damien was the presence of the Church for people who had been abandoned by everyone else. Have you experienced the gift of someone's ministry of charity? What would it look like for you to bring the presence of Christ and the Church into the lives of people who are suffering, lonely, or are gravely ill?
- Damien recognized that the people had tremendous needs on the physical and material levels (for example, medical attention, clean housing, safety, and beauty), and, as a priest, he could also see their need for the sacraments, counsel, and comfort. When you look around you, in your family and beyond, what physical, material, and spiritual needs do you see? Which of these needs can be met through the ministry of a priest? What would happen if you made that connection for someone?

Read ~::~ Reflect ~::~ Respond

The Anointing of the Sick can be received by those who suffer from serious illness and infirmity, and by those who are at the point of departing this life. This sacrament "completes our conformity to the death and Resurrection of Christ, just as Baptism began it" (CCC 1523). Learn about the effects of this sacrament by reading Exodus 40:9; Deuteronomy 31:6; Psalms 23:1–6; 107:20; 147:3; Acts 19:11–12; Colossians 1:24; *Catechism of the Catholic Church* 1503, 1505, 1520–1523, 1524, 1527, 1532.

Christ was touched by the suffering of those who approached him for healing. He took their pain upon himself and made it his own. Reflect on these accounts of healing in Scripture and deepen your understanding of the charism of healing in the Catechism by prayerfully reading Isaiah 53:4; 61:1; Luke 4:18; Matthew 9:20–22, 35; 25:36; Mark 2:9–12; Luke 10:2–37; John 9:6–7; Acts 10:38; 1 Peter 2:24; *Catechism of the Catholic Church* 1504–1509.

Saint Noël Chabanel

Holy Orders: Laying on of Hands

The Jesuit Noël Chabanel was a successful teacher of rhetoric who joined the other Jesuit missionaries ministering to the native peoples in New France. Because he was unable to learn even the basics of the Hurons' language and had difficulty adapting to their way of life, Father Chabanel could give little to the people he had come to serve. He constantly battled feelings of failure and spiritual desolation. He died at age thirty-six when he was ingloriously martyred at the hands of a disgruntled Huron. He is one of the North American martyrs.

Discussion Questions

~::~ What are some of the virtues that Noël Chabanel had to grow in as he struggled to be faithful to his call as a missionary among the native peoples in the New World? What struck you as he carried out his ministry?

~::~ The priest makes visible the presence of Christ in the midst of the community. Holy Orders "communicates a 'sacred power' which is none other than that of Christ" (CCC 1551). At the same time, the priest is not preserved from human weaknesses. How can realizing this be helpful in offering support to priests you know?

~::~ "Through the ordained ministry . . . the presence of Christ as head of the Church is made visible in the midst of the community of believers" (CCC 1549). What were the most illuminating parts of Noël Chabanel's story for understanding the various ways a priest makes Christ visible? How have you viewed the priesthood before reading the story? Is there anything different now about your understanding of the priesthood?

~::~ Noël Chabanel was faithful to his vocation despite the interior darkness he suffered throughout his missionary years. After reading his story, how does his faithfulness help you think differently about God's will as encompassing one's whole life and God's desire for all to be heirs of his divine life? How can Noël be a guide for you when difficulties and frustrations plague your best attempts at being faithful to your own vocation?

Read ~::~ Reflect ~::~ Respond

Missionary work requires patience. Proclaiming the Gospel to peoples and groups who do not believe in Christ is just the beginning. It is only slowly that the Church is able to permeate cultures and bring the people gradually into the fullness of Catholic life. Expand your appreciation of the Church's call to share the Gospel to the ends of the earth by reading Matthew 28:19; Mark 10:45; 2 Timothy 2:3–4; 1 Peter 2:5, 9; *Catechism of the Catholic Church* 456–460, 849–851, 854.

Through his ordination, the heart of the priest is universal, that is, prepared for a mission to preach the Gospel to the ends of the earth. Learn more about the role of the ordained minister in the life of the Church by reading John 4:34; 20:21–23; Mark 6:7, 12–13; 1 Peter 5:3; Hebrews 5:1–4; 7:17; *Catechism of the Catholic Church* 1548–1550, 1565–1566, 1568.

Saint Thomas Becket

Holy Orders: Laying on of Hands

Already a man of great integrity, as archbishop of Canterbury Thomas became a true man of God's Church. Although he did not seek the office, he corresponded to the graces of his ordination. The challenges of this office obliged him to stand against the will of his king and eventually face martyrdom.

Discussion Questions

- Either personally or through a book or movie, do you know of other stories of bishops and priests who have served the Church and given their lives for Christ and his people in defense of the Church? What inspires you most about them?

- Although Thomas Becket was a bishop, his conflict with Henry II left him tired, discouraged, and even pleading with the pope to be relieved of his responsibility. For any Christian trying to live as a disciple of Christ in public life, there will be conflict and struggle. The way forward will not always be clear or easy. Sometimes we may need to stand alone for what we believe to be right. After reading the life of Thomas Becket, have you discovered new sources of strength and courage?

- When King Henry II nominated Thomas Becket to be archbishop of Canterbury, Thomas immediately intensified his prayer and penance, as well as his generosity to the poor and suffering. He also opposed Henry's attempts to control the matters of the Church. How does this story add to your appreciation for the vocation and mission of those who are consecrated as bishops in the Church?

- ~::~ Which part of Thomas' story spoke to you most? What was the most surprising? What was the most challenging? What wisdom does the story of the life, ministry, and martyrdom of Thomas have for the Church today?

Read ~::~ Reflect ~::~ Respond

With his consecration, the bishop receives the grace to guide and defend the Church, the call to be a model in proclaiming the Gospel to everyone in his diocese, and the duty of giving preferential love to the sick and the poor. Consider the role of bishops today as you reflect on Matthew 16:19; 28:18–20; Romans 10:14–15; Ephesians 4:11–13; 2 Corinthians 4:1–6; Hebrews 13:17; *Catechism of the Catholic Church* 888–896, 1586.

The Holy Spirit directs the Church through a variety of hierarchic and charismatic gifts. The Church is the seed of the Kingdom of God on earth, and the Spirit impels her in her mission of establishing this Kingdom among all peoples. Reflect more deeply on the Church and the role of the hierarchy while reading John 3:16; 1 Corinthians 3:5–8; 2 Corinthians 4:7; Ephesians 4:11–13; 2 Timothy 1:5–14; 2:15; 4:7; Hebrews 13:7; *Catechism of the Catholic Church* 751–752, 765–766, 768, 1548–1553, 1558, 1560.

Saint Peter To Rot

Matrimony: Visible Sign of Christ's Love

As local catechist at the time of the Japanese military invasion, Peter found himself leader of his parish. He was the face of the Church to the invaders. With all his strength and ingenuity he nurtured the Church in hiding, and ultimately gave his life as a witness to faith and the sanctity of marriage.

Discussion Questions

~::~ The grace proper to the sacrament of Matrimony is intended to perfect the spouses' love and strengthen their unity. By this grace the husband and wife help one another to attain holiness and to welcome and raise children (see CCC 1641). What aspects of Peter and Paula's life together most illumines your own?

~::~ Peter To Rot was a loving and faithful husband and a devoted catechist. When the Japanese military forces invaded Papua New Guinea in the Second World War, eventually taking away all the missionaries, Peter, as the lay catechist, became the center of the Catholic community's life and ministry. What about his story illuminates the lay vocation in the Church? What challenges you personally? What have you found helpful for your living out of your lay vocation? Do any questions come to your mind?

~::~ What aspects of Peter and Paula's marriage especially ring true for you? What are signs of their maturing in holiness throughout the years of their marriage? Do the challenges they had in living their faith as a married couple speak to married couples today? In what ways?

Read ~::~ *Reflect* ~::~ *Respond*

Lay believers are "in the front line of Church life" (CCC 899). Just like all the members of the Church, they are entrusted with the evangelization of others, and in some cases their duty is most pressing because they are in situations, positions, and relationships where only they have the possibility and "means for permeating social, political, and economic realities with the demands of Christian doctrine and life" (CCC 899). Reflect on your own vocational response as a lay believer while reading Matthew 5:16; Romans 12:6–7; 1 Corinthians 12:27–29; 16:13; Ephesians 4:1; Colossians 3:17; 1 Peter 2:4–10; 2 Peter 1:5–7; *Catechism of the Catholic Church* 897–903, 905–906, 910, 1814, 1816.

God created out of love. He calls man and woman, who were created for one another, to live in love. And God himself seals the consent by which the spouses mutually give themselves to one another in marriage. In some quiet moments, allow God to deepen your appreciation for the beauty of the married life as you read Genesis 2:24; Matthew 19:4–6; 1 Corinthians 13:4–7; Ephesians 5:21, 25, 33; Romans 8:28; *Catechism of the Catholic Church* 1604–1606, 1638–1641, 1645.

Saint Zélie and Saint Louis Martin

Matrimony: The Domestic Church

Both Zélie and Louis Martin had desired to become religious consecrated to God, but God called them to the holy vocation of Marriage, where together with their children they created a holy family: their daughter Thérèse is a saint and doctor of the Church, and their daughter Leonie's cause for canonization was begun in 2015.

Discussion Questions

- In the story of Louis and Zélie Martin there are numerous examples of how deeply God was a part of every aspect of their relationship together and their family life. Have you experienced anything similar in your own family? Are any of the Martins' examples challenging to you? Have you had other experiences or developed practices of your own that build up Christian family life?

- Louis and Zélie Martin intentionally raised their family to be "holy ground," what today we would call a "domestic church." Today's families can imitate the Martins by making their own home a place where all members seek holiness together in the midst of everyday life, sufferings, and struggles. When you have read the story, what concrete suggestions can you give for building up the family as a domestic church?

- Each of us belongs to a family. In the story of Louis and Zélie Martin, what do you find helpful for understanding your own family experience?

~::~ Every family goes through its own dark valley of suffering. Has the story of Zélie and Louis illumined your own journey? As you reflect on their life experiences, what memories of your own journey arise? What would happen if you viewed life's daily events as reminders that your marriage or family is a place where God is present, where holiness grows and saints are made?

Read ~::~ Reflect ~::~ Respond

The sacrament of Matrimony perfects the human love of spouses, giving them "the grace to love each other with the love with which Christ has loved his Church" (CCC 1661). These graces of Matrimony make possible holiness of life, as may be seen by reading Romans 12:10; 13:8; 1 Corinthians 13:2; Ephesians 4:32; 5:25; Hebrews 10:24–25; 1 John 4:12, 16; 1 Peter 3:7; 2 Peter 1:5–7; *Catechism of the Catholic Church* 1601, 1639, 1641–1643, 1646, 1652–1653, 1656.

Families that are centers of living faith are of primary importance in bringing light to a world that is often hostile to the faith. The home, as "the domestic church," is the first place where children receive the proclamation of the faith and are brought up to live in a Christian way of life. Consider that God may be calling your family to be a beacon of light and living faith, as you reflect on your own experience and Genesis 1:28; 18:19; Deuteronomy 6:6–7; Psalms 127: 5, Proverbs 22:6; 1 Corinthians 13:4–7; 1 John 4:19; Colossians 3:13; *Catechism of the Catholic Church* 1655–1658, 1666.

Alphabetical Listing of Saints

Marie Paul Curley, FSP

When Sister Marie Paul Curley was a child, her imagination was captured by stories of the saints. That early fascination has continued throughout her religious life as a Daughter of St. Paul: she has written and produced numerous Catholic television programs on the saints for both children and adults. Her other books include *Eucharistic Adoration Prayer Book, Soul of Christ: Meditations on a Timeless Prayer,* and *Growing in Self-Esteem.* Currently Sister serves as an acquisition editor for Pauline Books & Media. You can find Sister Marie Paul online by visiting: www.pauline.org/mariepaulcurley.

Mary Lea Hill, FSP

Sister Mary Lea Hill, a member of the Daughters of St. Paul since 1964, has enjoyed communicating the faith through a variety of apostolic assignments. Her skills as a storyteller were honed as director of audiovisual productions when Pauline Books and Media first produced animated features in the early 1980s. An editor and author for many years, Sister Mary Lea has written a number of books, including *Growing in Virtue, One Vice at a Time: With a Crabby Mystic*; *Complaints of the Saints: Stumbling Upon Holiness with a Crabby Mystic*; *Blessed Are the Stressed: Secrets to a Happy Heart from a Crabby Mystic*; and the best-selling *Basic Catechism* (co-authored with Sister Susan Helen Wallace). Sister Mary Lea can be found on Instagram or Facebook as @crabbymystic.

Thank You.

Your purchase of this book and engagement with our other projects supports us in the work we do as Daughters of St. Paul. This book is the fruit of our consecrated life, prayer, and mission of communicating God's love.

We hold you and all your intentions in our prayers. We invite you to connect with us or send us prayer intentions at pauline.org.